The Promise of Peace

For God was pleased to have all his fullness dwell in him,
and through him to reconcile to himself all things,
whether things on earth or things in heaven,
by making peace through his blood, shed on the cross.

The Promise of Peace

A Unified Theory of Atonement

Alan J Spence

t&t clark

Published by T&T Clark
A Continuum imprint
The Tower Building, 11 York Road, London SE1 7NX
80 Maiden Lane, Suite 704, New York, NY 10038

www.continuumbooks.com

Chapter 1 of this book was originally published as 'A Unified Theory of the Atonement' in the International Journal of Systematic Theology, vol. 6, no. 4, October 2004 by Blackwell Publishing.

British Library Cataloguing-in-Publication Data
A catalogue record for this book is available from the British Library

Typeset by Fakenham Photosetting Limited, Fakenham, Norfolk
Printed on acid-free paper in Great Britain by Athenaeum Press Ltd, Gateshead, Tyne and Wear

ISBN 0 567 03117 9 (hardback)
ISBN 0 567 03118 7 (paperback)

for
Kingsley and Courteney

Contents

Acknowledgements

For over thirteen years I lived away from the world of academic theology, serving as a pastor to congregations in Zimbabwe and South Africa and being immersed in ecumenical issues, human rights advocacy and the establishment of a theological college. I am grateful to those friends who encouraged me to return to my books and try and clarify some of the ideas that have long played a part in my theological reflection. My thanks go to Norman Grimbeek, who has always had an over-generous view of my ability; to Douglas Knight who, along with his passion for theology, has a wonderful gift of hospitality; and to Taku Suda, a Japanese doctoral student at Cambridge, who shares my appreciation for the work of John Owen, and who at one time crossed the world simply to read a thesis on his christology.

Theology is of course best practised in dialogue with others. My theological community in years past and now again has centred on the Research Institute in Systematic Theology at King's College London, chaired formerly by the late Colin Gunton and now by Oliver Davies. The stimulation derived from the papers and discussions there has led many of us to engage more deeply with the central issues of theology. Particular thanks are due to those with whom I have argued passionately over lunch and beyond including: Lincoln Harvey, Paul Cummin, Chris Roberts, Justin Thacker, Sandra Fach and Steve Holmes.

Thanks also go to those who have read all or part of the draft of this book and given helpful comment, in particular to Murray Rae who has encouraged me to make some important changes, to Lucy Peppiott, Christine Morris, my brother Ian and of course my wife Sheila, who has done much more for me than improve my grammar.

Preface

Soon after its release in England, the journalist Polly Toynbee wrote a critical review of the film *The Lion, the Witch and the Wardrobe* in the *Guardian* (5 December 2005). Her article betrayed her deep anger with the Christian content of the film, particularly the moral implications arising from the death of the Christ-figure – Aslan the lion:

> Of all the elements of Christianity, the most repugnant is the notion of the Christ who took our sins upon himself and sacrificed his body in agony to save our souls. Did we ask him to? Poor child Edmund, to blame for everything, must bear the full weight of a guilt only Christians know how to inflict, with a twisted knife to the heart.

We catch in these words a glimpse of the animus which a major stream of secular, intellectual thought in Europe bears towards this traditional interpretation of the death of Christ. It is held to be repugnant, dangerous and manipulative.

What are Christians to make of this? There will be those who sympathize with Polly Toynbee's concerns and find themselves agreeing with her critique of C. S. Lewis's interpretation of the death of Christ. They may have asked themselves: Is there not something deeply immoral about the idea that an innocent man should die for our sins? What sort of God would approve of such a death? What sort of God would contrive it? Surely there must be less offensive ways to explain the significance of the cross? And they might well take comfort in the news that a fairly large section of the Church, notwithstanding its liturgy and hymnology, has already informally renounced the interpretation suggested in Lewis's book as being somewhat less than Christian.

In this I am reminded of an apocryphal story told of a group of German Jews who found themselves in a Nuremberg rally listening to an address by Adolf Hitler. So powerfully were they moved by his compelling rhetoric that when a mood of anti-Semitism swept across the stadium they rose as one with the vast crowd and joined the chant: 'Away with the Jews! Away with the Jews!' I am concerned that Christians may have been too quick to rise up and denounce an understanding of the death of Christ which has stood at the heart of the Church's faith for so long. It is my view that in doing so they are in danger of cutting their own spiritual lifeline.

How is one to come to a mind on such an issue? Our subjective experiences, although not without significance, have little persuasive force in debates of this kind. For instance, I personally find myself strangely drawn to one who gives over his life on my behalf and identify with this response from my hymn book:

My song is love unknown;
my saviour's love to me;
love to the loveless shown,
that they might lovely be.
O who am I,
that for my sake,
my Lord should take
frail flesh, and die?

Those who disagree with my position quite rightly point out that I, like others, am a product of a particular religious tradition. Samuel Crossman, the seventeenth-century English Protestant who wrote these words, was influenced by the theology of the Reformation. But can we be sure that the Reformers were right? Perhaps they were overly dependent on ideas that derived from Luther's personal experience of religious anxiety? Was Luther himself not unhelpfully influenced by a low view of human ability that he derived from Augustine? Did Augustine, in turn, ever discard the Manichaean dualism of his earlier years?

Although such a cursory dismissal of these major voices in Christian thought is simplistic and unwarranted, the shift of subject matter from subjective experience to the development of ideas is in fact quite helpful. The material we are being asked to consider is now part of the public domain. We have, as it were, entered a room in which a conversation is taking place. Articulate voices are engaged in a fascinating and sometimes heated discussion about the significance of the death and resurrection of Jesus Christ in the light of the Church's normative documents. The conversation has continued, with some major breaks, for nearly two thousand years. As with a video recording we can turn back to almost any stage of the discussion, listen to the relevant arguments, weigh up their strengths and weaknesses and determine for ourselves whether their conclusions are justified. By so engaging with the conversation in this way we can try and follow its course, understanding why it has chosen the particular routes it has.

I enter that metaphorical room with deep concerns about the direction that the conversation has taken in more recent years. It seems to me that at significant points the Church has been persuaded to embark on paths which are unhelpful, if not mistaken. I would like to look more closely at the arguments and analyses that have led to such decisions and test their coherence. It means that this book is polemical in nature. The focus on areas of dispute, however, should not conceal my agreement with the greater part of the theology of many of the principal figures in this debate.

I also come into the room hoping to contribute positively to the discussion. The atonement is a subject that has for a long time both fascinated and bewildered me with its complexity, depth and significance. It is not surprising that so many of the Church's best minds have wrestled long and hard to clarify its meaning. Yet having been enriched by their work and awed by their wisdom, I still find myself returning to the biblical witness itself, in the hope that it might disclose more of the inner rationality of its message. Anselm spoke of the need to believe in order to understand, but it seems to me that along with belief are the hard requirements of patience, integrity and a degree of freedom from the conclusions of others.

In defending my thesis, I trust that this study will also uncover something of the mystery of God's redemptive logic – the coherence of his eternal purpose to reconcile a people to himself, what we might call 'the rationality of the atonement'.

A Normative Theory of Atonement

The big question

There is a suspicion abroad that academic theologians prefer to focus on the little questions. They will argue with quiet authority about the minutiae of biblical studies whether it be the meaning of an obscure Aramaic word or the reliability of a phrase attributed to Jesus, but be somewhat embarrassed and reticent to offer a frank answer when faced with the classical questions of the Christian faith, such as, 'Why did God become man?' It is widely assumed that such a question has the same logical status as a query about which type of grapes produce the best wine. There is no single objective answer. Some people prefer one variety, some another. In fact, it is the mixing or blending of grapes that produces many of the world's most superb wines. It is felt that the same is probably true in soteriology, the doctrine of salvation. There is no master-story, no $e = mc^2$, no rich, single account through which the multi-faceted work of Christ may be coherently held together. But why such pessimism? I know of no compelling theological reason why Christians should not at least try to provide a clear and straightforward answer to important questions. The aim of this chapter is to take some preparatory steps on the path to forming such a 'master-story' or 'unified theory of the atonement', one that will help disclose a coherent relationship between the various soteriological motifs.

Theories of salvation

This is of course not an original project. The question posed above is derived from the title of Anselm's classical and widely influential work on the atonement *Cur Deus Homo*. As to the analysis and comparison of the various soteriological themes, Gustav Aulén's pioneer study *Christus Victor: an historical study of the three main types of the idea of the Atonement* has provided a helpful classification that brings some order to the discussion. As suggested in his title, Aulén discerned three basic atonement types. He argued that alongside the objectivist Latin model of atonement related to the work of Anselm, in which satisfaction is required by divine holiness and justice, or the subjectivist interpretation suggested by Abelard, where the emphasis lies on the change in human attitudes towards God, there is a third, generally neglected, soteriological type in which the central theme is that of victory over the oppressive forces ranging against humankind. In this intentionally dualistic perspective the tyrannies that hold men and women in bondage and need to be overcome by God are seen to include the devil and his demons, the principalities and powers, death, sin and the law. Aulén showed that this 'dramatic' model underlies much of the soteri-ology of the Fathers, particularly of Irenaeus, Bishop of Lyons, and that Luther was also largely dependent on it. Although he demonstrated that this idea influenced the thought of the New Testament writers, he was less persuasive in showing that it was the only or even dominant model in their exposition of Christ's work.

What is of interest to us in the present discussion is not just Aulén's division of the various soteriological themes into three basic types, but his analysis of their structure and inner logic. He argued that each model operates as a fairly independent network of ideas with its own particular interpretation of sin, salvation, the incarnation and conception of God. It is an interesting thesis that I believe could be fruitfully developed. I would like to press forward, at least to begin with, along the path that he has opened.

What is the most useful way among the various possibilities to classify the different atonement types? Colin Gunton in *The Actuality of the Atonement* categorized the soteriological theories according to the contexts of the central biblical metaphors that generated them: the battlefield, the law-courts and the altar. His intention was not to contrast and compare these ideas but to show how together they might refer effectively to an external, objective reality accomplished by Christ. My own classification has an eye to the resolution that Christ brings to the human predicament. Here then, developing Aulén, is a summary of the main soteriological types with an outline of their inner structure.

Jesus Christ as Victor

He is the one who overcomes the dark powers opposing humankind. These oppressive forces may include sin, death, the law, the devil, the principalities and powers. A deep dualism lies at the heart of this interpret-ative scheme. The language tends to be militaristic and confrontational, dependent on ideas such as authority, power and victory. As to the person of Christ, the emphasis is on his divine action directed towards these alien forces defeating them in the cross. His resurrection is the central event of history, manifesting Christ's triumph and lordship.

Jesus Christ as Mediator

He is the one who reconciles God and his people. The various aspects of the human predicament are all derived from the central problem of estrangement from God. The perspective is monotheistic and any indication of dualism is greatly modified. The principal motifs are divine mercy and the forgiveness of sin along with human repentance and faith. As to the person of Christ, the emphasis is on his assumption of human form. The focus is on his life of obedience as man directed towards God, thus representing fallen humankind. The cross is the pivotal historical event, where Christ is generally held to have played a representative or substitutionary role. The resurrection is God's justification of Christ's person and ministry.

Jesus Christ as Exemplar

He is the one who demonstrates the love of God and thereby transforms our attitudes towards God, ourselves and the world. The human predicament is understood in terms of sinfulness, fear, helplessness and angst, all aspects of the inner, marred, human condition. This model, sometimes described as subjective, is generally upheld as the principal atonement type by those who seek an alternative to the objectivist views of Christ's work suggested in the two models above. The divinity of Christ is not essential in some variations of the theory, while the self-giving and identification with human suffering demonstrated in the cross is generally given priority over the resurrection. Superficially related to this third model, but quite different in operation, is the understanding of Christ as God's revelation, a revelation considered to be a transformative objective reality.

We can consider these various models as interpretative theories of the raw biblical material on salvation. Are they complementary theories? Because they each refer to biblical themes, it is tempting to suppose that together they might somehow form one comprehensive and coherent account. But a closer examination of how they operate in practice indicates that these models, as distinct from the atonement metaphors, function as competing theories. For example, few would want to deny that the life and death of Christ is a demonstration of God's love. But the exemplarist model is not merely an emphasis on God's love in Christ. Rather, it has been put forward as an alternative theory by those who have difficulties with other models: the victory model's dependence on a mythological interpretation of reality and the mediation model's use of a problematic penal theory and a superstitious view of sacrificial efficacy. Similarly, the first two models maintain quite different positions on dualism, the human predicament, the effect of sin and, to some extent, the person of Christ. As we analyse their operation we discover that they provide what seem to be mutually exclusive ways of interpreting the whole framework of concepts that relate to human salvation.

Now if these are indeed competing theories how does one decide between them? The success of a theory is generally considered to lie in its ability to give a natural and coherent account of the material which it seeks to interpret and to be illuminating or fruitful in wider application. Conversely, theories tend to be discarded if excessive tinkering or manipulation of the base material is required for them to 'fit'. A good starting point then is to ask 'which of these models serves as the most natural interpretative tool of the biblical material?' There is a current debate in Pauline studies which will, I believe, shed light on this question even as our question serves to illuminate that discussion.

The New Perspective

Bishop N. T. Wright is a leading figure in a movement in New Testament studies known as the 'New Perspective' on Paul. It is a concern of his and others to correct what is believed to be the false track taken by Protestant theologians in interpreting the meaning of 'justification by faith' since the time of Luther.

The heart of the debate has to do with a contrast made in Paul's writings between justification by faith and by works of the law. Reformed theologians have interpreted this as indicating a distinction between divine grace and human effort as ways to experience salvation. No one will earn justification by their obedience to God's requirements because such perfect obedience is not forthcoming.[1] Only as men and women wholeheartedly trust or believe in Jesus Christ are they accounted righteous by God as an act of grace. Wright sees the matter quite differently. The distinction for him has nothing to do with an ahistorical concern of how we become Christians. It has to do, rather, with the indicators or markers of membership in God's covenant family, of who will be justified on the last day. The Jews believed that a number of their practices including circumcision, Sabbath observance and their refusal to eat pork effectively marked them off from the Gentile community and showed them to be children of the covenant. Paul, according to Wright, argues that the true indicator of the people of God or the family of Abraham is faith. Paul's difficulty with the Jews had to do with their failure to recognize the breadth of the covenant and the extent of the membership of God's people. The markers they looked to were still the works of the law rather than faith.

The interpretation of this Pauline contrast between justification by works of the law and by faith is not the be-all and end-all of the debate, but it is

[1]C. E. B. Cranfield, *The Epistle to the Romans*, vol. 1, The International Critical Commentary on the Holy Scriptures of the Old and New Testaments (Edinburgh, T&T Clark Ltd, 1980), p. 198.

a shibboleth which clearly distinguishes the protagonists. Why does this apparently esoteric discussion become a matter of such great issue? It is, as I see it, at least in part because we have here a critical point of confrontation between the two quite different models of salvation which we have designated by the terms 'victor' and 'mediator'. Let us consider how these models operate in the discussion.

Victory as an interpretative tool

In his interpretation of Paul's writings Wright's soteriology fits fairly neatly into what we have described as the 'victor' model of atonement. In his book *What St Paul Really Said*[2] he identifies the oppressive forces facing humankind as 'the principalities and powers', the enslaving force of the 'elements of the world', sin and death (see pp. 47, 48). Wright affirms that 'victory' is his preferred soteriological motif and believes that this perspective is able to give a full account of the meaning of the crucifixion.

> For this reason I suggest that we give priority – a priority among equals, perhaps, but still a priority – to those Pauline expressions of the crucifixion of Jesus which describe it as the decisive victory over the 'principalities and powers'. Nothing in the many other expressions of the meaning of the cross is lost if we put this in the centre (p. 47).

Within this perspective evil and sin tend to be viewed along with other dark forces as objective entities determining and in some sense external to the human condition. They can be conquered and dealt with by the cross.

> At the heart of Paul's gospel there stands the claim that the death of Jesus the king had defeated evil at its very heart (p. 52).

Consistent with this model, Jesus' ministry is viewed by Wright principally in terms of his power, authority and lordship. The proclamation of the gospel is consequently the proclamation of the lordship of Christ. The ideas of the righteousness of God and justification by faith are not considered by him to be part of the gospel (p. 94). For Wright these are matters of ecclesiology rather than soteriology. The content of the gospel is clearly summarized in Romans 1. 4, 5 (p. 126). It is the declaration by the Spirit of Jesus' divine sonship through the resurrection. By means of this announcement God converts the hearers of the gospel and brings them into the family.

> Paul discovered, at the heart of his missionary practice, that when he announced the lordship of Jesus Christ, the sovereignty of King Jesus, this very announcement was the means by which the living God reached out with his love and changed the hearts and lives of men and women, forming them into a community of love across traditional

---

[2] Tom Wright, *What St Paul Really Said* (Oxford, Lions Publishing, 1997).

barriers, liberating them from the paganism which had held them captive, enabling them to become, for the first time, the truly human beings they were meant to be (p. 61).

If the lordship of Christ is the heart of the gospel message in the victory model, it follows that the appropriate response demanded of the hearer is allegiance to his person and obedience to his commands.

> The royal proclamation is not simply the conveying of true information about the kingship of Jesus. It is the putting into effect of that kingship, the decisive and authoritative summoning to allegiance (p. 61).

A mediatorial paradigm

Now Wright's use of 'victory' as an interpretative scheme for the early chapters of Romans is remarkable, for the whole structure and content of the text appears to exhibit all the classic features of the mediator theory.

First, in the mediatorial model the predicament facing men and women is not considered to be an array of external, secondary powers or forces but, because of what they have done, God himself – God as judge. As we approach the text of Romans it is useful to remind ourselves that there is a general aversion to the concepts of God's condemnation, wrath or judgement in much of modern religious consciousness. We need, therefore, to be particularly careful not to be blinkered by the current prevailing perspective, but look carefully, particularly in the passages preceding Paul's explication of justification, to see whether such a presentation of the human predicament is in fact present.

> The wrath of God is being revealed from heaven against all the godlessness and wickedness of men (1. 18). Now we know that God's judgement against those who do such things is based on truth (2. 2) ... do you think you will escape God's judgement? (2. 3) ... you are storing up wrath for yourself for the day of God's wrath, when his righteous judgement will be revealed (2. 5). But for those who are self-seeking and who reject the truth and follow evil there will be wrath and anger. (2. 8) ... all who sin under the law will be judged by the law (2. 12). This will take place on the day when God will judge men's secrets through Jesus Christ, as my gospel declares (2. 16) ... so that every mouth may be silenced and the whole world held accountable to God (3. 19). Since we have now been justified by his blood, how much more shall we be saved from God's wrath (5. 9)?

Running right through this portrayal of the human predicament and so highlighting its severity is a persistent warning addressed to both Gentile and Jewish reader. 'You, therefore, have no excuse ...'(2. 1). 'Do you think you will escape God's judgment?' (2. 3). 'Now you, if you call yourself a Jew ... Do you dishonour God by breaking the law?' (2. 17, 23). The literary form of this section is not that of a seminar on ecclesiology but rather of an evangelist's sermon aiming to undermine the religious self-assurance of his hearers. (Compare this with Matthew's account of John the Baptist's preaching. Matt 3. 7–10.)

Second, it is against this dark and awful backdrop of the righteous condemnation or judgement of God on human perversity that the motif of mediation highlights the Father's gracious love in Christ. Jesus is God's agent to effect reconciliation and bring peace, demonstrating God's love to those who are still enemies. The metaphors generally used in the model of mediation include those of redemption, sacrifice, propitiation and expiation. And it is precisely this group of concepts that we find in the key atonement passage in Romans 3.

> ... and are justified freely by his grace through the redemption that came by Christ Jesus. God presented him as a sacrifice of atonement (propitiation) through faith in his blood (vv. 24, 25).

Elsewhere in the epistle Paul underlines this general dependence on sacrificial terminology. 'He was delivered over to death for our sins and was raised to life for our justification' (4. 25). ' ... by sending his own Son in the likeness of sinful man to be a sin offering' (8. 3).

Third, the content of the gospel is thus understood as an account of the work of the cross and the forgiveness that flows from it. It is significant that elsewhere in the corpus when Paul uses the word 'gospel' and gives an explanation of its meaning it has to do with the message of the cross and the reconciliation won by Christ's death. (see 1 Cor 1. 17, 18; Col 1. 21–3). It seems far more natural to interpret Romans 1. 3, 4 christologically rather than soteriologically as in the prior model. This passage indicates the twofold perspective by which Jesus' person is to be understood. 'As to his human nature a descendant of David, and who through the Spirit of holiness was declared with power to be the Son of God' (Rom 1. 3, 4a). The 'gospel' in Romans is recognized as being summarized not here but in the concepts of the righteousness of God and justification as outlined in 1. 16, 17 and 3. 21–6. These passages might not offer a detailed explanation of how to become a Christian, but they are a summary of what God has done to reconcile his people to himself. Paul's own explanation of justification apart from works in chapter four indicates that this concept functions in a manner similar to the idea of forgiveness.

> David says the same thing when he speaks of the blessedness of the man to whom God credits righteousness apart from works: Blessed are they whose transgressions are forgiven, whose sins are covered. Blessed is the man whose sin the Lord will never count against him. (Rom 4. 6, 7).

Fourth, we saw above that in the victory paradigm the proclamation of the lordship of Christ demands obedience and allegiance from the hearers. But when Christ is understood as the mediator who brings reconciliation, the immediate call on the hearer is to turn from sin, to trust and believe. Faith is the principal characteristic required as the appropriate response to the gospel of reconciliation and the discussion of this theme in the fourth chapter bears witness to the central place this concept plays in Paul's exposition.

Finally, the relation of Christ's person to his saving ministry is indicated most clearly in the fifth chapter where Christ is portrayed as a second Adam, who through his obedience to God brings life and justification. This is contrasted with the first man who through his disobedience brought death and condemnation to the world. The focus is on Christ's work as man towards God, the typical mediatorial direction.

It would seem that in almost all its features the first section of Romans lends itself naturally to a 'mediatorial' reading. The emphasis on divine judgement as the predicament facing both Jews and Gentiles, the use of legal and sacrificial metaphors, the interpretation of the gospel in terms of forgiveness, the focus on faith and the ministry of Christ as man towards God, are all explicit in the biblical material and are naturally bound together in the structure of ideas that constitute the atonement type that we have characterized by 'Jesus as Mediator'. The overwhelming presumption is that the concepts of 'justification' and 'the righteousness of God' are most appropriately interpreted within the framework of grace, forgiveness and the removal of enmity. The concern about membership of God's family and how that membership is marked does not flow obviously from the text, and if it is implied, it is quite secondary to the concern about how Jews and Gentiles who justly stand together under divine judgement are acquitted by God.

This comparison of Wright's use of a victory model of salvation with that of mediation in interpreting Romans illustrates how these models operate as comparatively self-contained and independent soteriological theories. The principal features of each model require the other related features to form a coherent system. But, conversely, they also tend to preclude the features of the alternate model. We should not be surprised that the concepts of reconciliation, mercy and forgiveness are almost totally neglected in Wright's account.

Arguments for a new perspective

Now if the model of 'victory' simply does not work as an interpretative tool why does Wright use it? What *external* factors incline him to discard the traditional Protestant exposition of justification with the framework of ideas and inner logic that the mediation theory suggests? The overall purpose of the text, the place of faith in salvation and the nature of Jewish religion at the time Paul wrote all play a part in influencing Wright's interpretative scheme. This is my summary of his concerns.

1. If we start with a Reformed interpretation of justification, 'Paul's discussion of Israel and its Torah either takes second place or, worse, is relegated to a more abstract and generalized discussion of the sin and salvation of humans in general, in which the question of Israel's fate is essentially a side issue'.[3]
2. The Reformed understanding of justification tends towards an inordinate focus on private faith and its efficacy, in which faith is considered as meriting salvation.
3. It has been shown by Sanders and others that the Judaism of Paul's time was not a religion of legalistic works righteousness. It is not right, therefore, to interpret Paul's theory of justification as implying that the Jews were seeking to secure salvation through works of the law.

What is the strength of these arguments? Do they singly or together warrant the rejection of a traditional Protestant interpretation of justification along with the use of a mediatorial model of salvation?

1. This is the easiest point to deal with for it begs the question. We cannot dismiss a particular interpretative framework because it does not lead us to our preferred conclusion or balance of themes. The question, 'What are the central issues in Romans?' can only be answered after the honest exposition has been done. Our analysis of the subtle and complex interdependence of Paul's various concerns in determining his overall purpose in the letter must wait till the end and not be used to prescribe our interpretation of the text.
2. Wright is deeply concerned that the role of faith in the saving process is misunderstood in the Reformed tradition. 'The place of faith in this picture has long been problematic within post-Reformation dogmatics. Is faith something I "do" to earn God's favour, and, if not, what role does it play?' (*What St Paul Really Said*, p. 125). 'This faith was not something Abraham "did" in order to earn the right to be within the people of God. It was the badge that showed that he was a member – indeed, the founding member – of that people' (p. 130). ' "Faith", for Paul, is therefore not a substitute "work" in a moralistic sense. It is not something one does in order to gain admittance into the covenant people' (p. 132).

Wright is insistent that faith is not to be considered as something that I 'do' in order to earn salvation. Faith would then become some sort of substitute work. It is not to be understood as a precondition to becoming a Christian. Faith is rather a badge or marker that we have become Christians. Wright's concerns are understandable. His alternate theory is, however, highly problematic.

[3] N. T. Wright, *The Letter to the Romans: Introduction, Commentary and Reflection*, The New Interpreter's Bible, A Commentary in Twelve Volumes, vol. X (Nashville, Abingdon Press, 2002), p. 403.

First, the question about whether faith can save is not an issue that first arose in post-Reformation dogmatics. In the Epistle of James the matter is raised with clear reference to Paul's contrast between justification by faith and by works of the law. 'What good is it my brothers, if a man claims to have faith but has not deeds? Can such a faith save him?' (2. 14). Right from the start Paul is being interpreted as arguing for faith as the way of securing salvation as opposed to deeds. This passage counts decisively against Wright's thesis that Paul's contrast of works of the law and faith has nothing to do with attaining salvation.

Second, Wright appears to have created a straw man. Reformed theology has always insisted that faith does not of itself earn salvation or merit God's favour. Salvation is won solely through the work of Christ. The gift of salvation is from start to finish a product of divine grace. It comes to those who look not to themselves but to God alone. This 'looking to God alone for salvation' is the essence of faith. To trust in the act of faith or to consider the human response to grace as in some way meritorious, although a possibility, is always a distortion or perversion of faith. It turns attention away from God and back to human achievement. But faith properly conceived as a 'looking to God alone' or 'trusting in his promises' is the 'channel', so to speak, of divine grace and salvation for the individual. In that sense it is necessary for salvation. Although faith is a divine gift, it is thus not merely a marker or badge of those who have received salvation. It is much more than that. Faith is the instrument through which salvation and its benefits are experienced.

Third, it is difficult to envisage a New Testament idea that is supported by a more widespread biblical testimony than this. Seven times in the key justification passage of Rom 3. 21–31 alone the instrumental nature of faith in Christ is emphasized. Wright's somewhat forced solution is to translate three of these occurrences in terms of the faithfulness of Christ (p. 128). But his problem is rather like that of the man who began to remove the heads from a number of daffodils in an attempt to deny the advent of spring. There are just too many of them! Surely even the most determined of polemicists must concede that the biblical testimony to the instrumental role of faith in salvation is both widespread and unambiguous. 'Does God give you his Spirit and work miracles among you by observing the law, or by your believing what you heard? So also Abraham 'believed God, and it was credited to him as righteousness. Understand, then, that those who have faith are children of Abraham' (Gal 3. 5–7).

Wright's development of the 'merely a marker theory' of faith arises then out of his concern that faith should not be considered as meritorious, as earning salvation and therefore as a new form of works righteousness. Dependent on this is his theory that justification is 'how you can tell who is a member of the covenant family' (p. 122). This is quite different from recognizing it as the divine act which reverses the state of condemnation under which all men and women find themselves.[4] This reinterpretation of justification as a matter of ecclesiological recognition rather than of soteriological determination requires a decisive movement away from the mediatorial framework of ideas and leads to the adoption of an alternative theory of salvation. In short, Wright's difficulties with an instrumental understanding of faith contributes to his use of the victory model.

3. The argument from the historical context is strongly made: Recent studies have shown that Judaism in Paul's time was not a form of legalistic works-righteousness. Paul, consequently, would not have criticised the Jews of his day for seeking to earn divine favour through some form of legalism. To interpret 'works of the law' in Pauline literature as implying a legalistic approach to salvation is thus to transpose categories more appropriate to Luther's controversy with medieval Catholicism back into the New Testament texts. We need to unpack the ideas contained in this somewhat dense argument if we are to clarify the issues.

E. P. Sanders has shown from the literature of Paul's time that Jews believed that 'obedience maintains one's position in the covenant, but it does not earn God's grace as such'.[5] Grace is rather freely given the Jews through their election into the covenant. Even this brief summary is not unchallenged. Francis Watson in a recent paper 'Not the New Perspective' has argued that in the Judaism of Paul's time, grace and obedience cannot be as easily separated as Sanders's position suggests.

> This overlooks the fact that the Law given at Sinai is *both* the expression of the divine election of Israel *and* the divine demand for Israel's obedience. The Torah is simultaneously gift and demand, the embodiment of the two-sided covenant principle which states not only that 'I will be their God' but also that 'they shall be my people'. Israel *must* live as the elect people, thereby fulfilling its side of the covenant; and that means that Israel must live by the Torah.

[4] There are times when Wright's interpretation of justification appears far closer to the Reformed tradition than is suggested in this quotation from *What St Paul Really Said*. In his commentary on Romans he says of it: 'It is God's declaration that those who believe are in the right; their sins have been dealt with; they are God's true covenant people, God's renewed humanity.' (*The Letter to the Romans*, p. 471.) Nevertheless the distinction with the Reformed tradition is maintained if we see Wright as holding that justification is an act of recognition of a reality that has already taken place in the believer, rather than one that transforms the status of the person who has faith. However, in a reply to the evangelical Australian bishop Paul Barnet, posted on the Internet, Wright used this expression of justification: 'This present declaration constitutes all believers as the single people, the one family promised to Abraham' (N. T. Wright, *The Shape of Justification*, www.angelfire.com/mi2/paulpage/Shape.html). But if justification *constitutes* the people of God it seems difficult to deny that it also transforms their status before God. If so, Wright's argument with the Reformed tradition collapses, for justification is then a matter of soteriology and not just ecclesiology.

[5] E. P. Sanders, *Paul and Palestinian Judaism: A Comparison of Patterns of Religion* (London, SCM Press, 1977) p. 430.

There is, then, no divine election or covenant that precedes or relativizes the Torah. Covenant and Torah are indistinguishable.[6]

Nevertheless, for the sake of the discussion let us accept the position that grace was an integral aspect of contemporary Judaism in Paul's time. Why would it be inappropriate to put to these Jews the warning that salvation is not to be attained by moral effort or legal obedience? Wright's response is that such an argument implies the existence of a type of Pelagianism, a system which holds that salvation can be obtained by human effort, an option that the ordinary Jew would never have considered. In fact, Wright suggests that it is such an implausible concept that it is unlikely that anyone today would defend it.

> There is simply no way human beings can make themselves fit for the presence or salvation of God. What is more I know of no serious theologian, Protestant, Catholic or Orthodox, who thinks otherwise.... If Pelagius survives at all today, it is at the level of popular secular moralism, which is in any case becoming harder and harder to find in the Western world (*What St Paul Really Said*, p. 116).

Wright's net has too large a mesh to catch the fish of human self-righteousness. Of course almost no one would argue for the position he has described. But, and this is the remarkable irony, Wright, as we have just seen above, was concerned about the Reformed understanding of faith precisely because he discerned in it a reliance on 'faith' as a human 'work' to attain divine favour – and this in a community which speaks endlessly about grace. We are told that the proper context of the polemic about faith and 'works of the law' is Luther's confrontation with medieval Catholicism. Yet, are we to believe that Catholic theology at that time was devoid of any principle of grace or that anyone was actually arguing that you could gain eternal salvation wholly by human effort? Self-righteousness, a looking to what you have done as the foundation of your own assurance before God, does not mean formally embracing a Pelagian theological system.[7] It is a far more subtle and elusive creature than that. We need a deeper insight to uncover it.

Luke recounts a parable of Jesus. 'To some who were confident of their own righteousness and looked down on everybody else, Jesus told this parable: "Two men went up to the temple to pray, one a Pharisee and the other a tax collector"' (Luke 18. 9, 10). The paradox in the parable is that the man who was most effusive in his thanksgiving and apparent recognition of grace is the man who returned home unjustified. There

---

[6]Francis Watson, 'Not the New Perspective', an unpublished paper delivered at the British New Testament Conference, Manchester, September 2001.

[7]It is interesting that Pelagius believed that baptism was a regenerative and so gracious act. To be a Pelagian does not require a total denial of grace. See J. N. D. Kelly, *Early Christian Doctrines*, 5th edn, (London, Adam & Charles Black, 1977) p. 357.

was nothing wrong with his theology, his self-assured attitude was the problem.[8] And this focus on the individual's motivation, the intentions of the heart, is not to be dismissed as an ahistorical relapse into Lutheran piety, it lies rather at the centre of Jesus' consistent affirmation of the humble as heirs of the kingdom and his damning critique of the proud.

In short, first-century Judaism as a theological system might well have had important gracious features, but there is no reason why it, along with many Christian theological traditions with tendencies towards self-righteousness or legalism, did not need to be confronted with the argument that 'all of our best deeds will not of themselves earn God's approval'. The interpretation of 'works of the law' as a summary of all that leads to the presumption to righteousness and more that is suggested in the second and third chapters of Romans, cannot simply be thrown out on the basis that it is an inappropriate message to the Jews of that time. Human nature being what it is, they are unlikely to have been very different from us.[9] And this is the vital point. This is a message not merely for the Jews but for the whole world. As Paul reminds us in the climactic conclusion to his courtroom argument, Jews and Gentiles are indicted together under the same charge in the one dock.

> Now we know that whatever the law says, it says to those who are under the law, so that every mouth may be silenced and the whole world held accountable to God. Therefore no one will be declared righteous in his sight by observing the law ... (or more literally, 'no one will be justified by works of the law') (Rom 3. 19, 20).

Summary

Following Aulén we have classified the various soteriological themes into three basic types that operate as distinctive interpretative theories of the raw biblical material. Each has its own inner logic and particular presentation of key theological concepts. They might look like complementary models, yet an analysis of their structure and operation shows that they function in practice as competing theories.

The competitive nature of the theories has been illustrated in the brief survey of Wright's alternative proposal to the standard Reformed

---

[8] To undermine the traditional interpretation of Paul it is insufficient to demonstrate that Palestinian Judaism as a religious system gave priority to God's electing grace rather than to the requirement to obey the law. It must also be shown that the great majority of its adherents gave such priority to God's grace over the demands of the law in their own religious motivation. This will not be easy to do for sadly our attitudes tend to lag behind our theology.

[9] Jesus' critique of the self-righteousness of the Pharisees and the hypocrisy of Jewish religious leaders remains pertinent today because we share together in the failings of the human condition. Who of us has not come across church office-bearers who delight in their titles, places of honour, clerical dress and other indicator of religious status? Who of us has not shared in their conceit? (see Matt 23).

interpretation of justification by faith. He used the victory model of salvation to expound the soteriological themes of Romans, consistently interpreting its central concepts within the framework of that theory. The fact that mediatorial ideas such as enmity, guilt, reconciliation, forgiveness and mercy are almost wholly absent in his interpretation is an indication of the determinative and exclusive nature of the model. There is in it no need for forgiveness, because the predicament facing us has to do not with the person of God, but a consortium of external powers; Christ has come then not to make peace with God, but to overcome these alien forces; his ministry is not understood in terms of his identification with humanity and representation of us before the Father but as the divine conqueror of his and our enemies. The difficulty with such a model, particularly when it is used to interpret Romans, is, as we have seen, that it just does not do justice to the material before it. It does not give an adequate account of what is clearly there. Too much has to be discounted. Too many features are imported. Too often the text has to be manipulated to make it conform to an alien logic.

Victory as a comprehensive account

Yet it is not always the case that a theologian embracing the victory model feels it is necessary to ignore or sideline the key mediatorial themes. Aulén, who also championed this 'dramatic' type, believed that they might be embraced within his system. For him the victory model was not just a theory of salvation from hostile powers, it also offered an explanation of how there could be reconciliation with God.

> It is important above all, at this point to see clearly that this work of salvation and deliverance is at the same time a work of atonement, of reconciliation between God and the world. It is altogether misleading to say that the triumph of Christ over the powers of evil, whereby He delivers man, is a work of salvation but not of atonement; for the two ideas cannot possibly be thus separated. It is precisely the work of salvation wherein Christ breaks the power of evil that constitutes the atonement between God and the world; for it is by it that He removes the enmity, takes away the judgement which rested on the human race, and reconciles the world to Himself, not imputing to them their trespasses.[10]

It is a bold idea, but how substantial is Aulén's claim that this model with its theme of divine victory over evil powers can help us to understand and explain the process of reconciliation? Can the removal of enmity and condemnation be understood wholly within the framework of the

---

[10] Gustav Aulén, *Christus Victor: An historical study of the three main types of the idea of the Atonement,* trans. by A. G. Hebert (London, SPCK, 1978), p. 71.

defeat of evil? It is far from clear that it can. Reconciliation implies a prior relationship of estrangement and hostility; that some sort of personal conflict or antagonism exists between the parties. Enmity and the resulting judgement are not, as Aulén suggests, external oppressive forces but descriptions of inner broken relations between God and humankind. Concepts such as grace, repentance and forgiveness appear more appropriate in this context than those of triumph and victory. Aulén never goes on to help us understand how the battle motif, so helpful in explaining the experience of human freedom and liberation, is able to shed light on the problems of guilt, judgement and animosity.

Mediation as a normative theory

If the victory model does not seem able to serve as an overarching theory of salvation, what of the mediatorial model? Can it offer a comprehensive account of why God became man? Is it able within its own system of ideas to give an adequate explanation of the biblical motifs linked with victory?

The classical expression of Christ's triumph over death comes towards the conclusion of Paul's argument for the resurrection of the dead in 1 Corinthians. 'When the perishable has been clothed with the imperishable, and the mortal with immortality, then the saying that is written will come true: "Death has been swallowed up in victory." "Where, O death, is your victory? Where, O death, is your sting?"' (1 Cor 15. 54, 55).

The victory model offers a straightforward interpretation of this passage. Death as an oppressive force standing against humankind is defeated or overwhelmed by Christ's divine power through his resurrection. Such an unambiguous presentation of the theme of victory seems of itself to undermine any hope of a unified theory of atonement. For how can we hold together this triumphant account of Christ's resurrection with the narrative of Jesus as a man like us offering himself up through the eternal Spirit as a sacrifice to God? (see Heb 9. 14).

Before we despair of forming a unified soteriology, let us look a little more closely at Paul's account above of the defeat of death. A victory perspective tends to consider death as an entity in its own right. Proud and arrogant it stands against God, and as an enemy force holds humanity in its unremitting grasp. It is finally put to the sword or overthrown by the divine power of Christ manifest in the resurrection. But such poetic language must not mislead us about Paul's theology of death. He does not consider it to be an independent force opposing God. Death, for Paul, came into the world through human sin and is ultimately related to divine judgement (see Rom 5). Sin and death are thus inextricably linked in his thought? 'For sin, seizing the opportunity afforded by the commandment, deceived me, and through the commandment put me to death' (Rom 7. 11).

The recognition of this link between death and sin changes everything. Death is the external indication of a deeper problem, that is, the poison of sin. And sin is not to be overcome by obedience to divine requirements, for the law merely gives power to sin. Sin is dealt with in the first place through atonement, through the grace manifest in the mediatorial death of Christ. That is why Paul's twofold question 'Where, O death, is your victory? Where, O death, is your sting?' must not be interpreted rhetorically. It does have an answer and Paul provides it. 'The sting of death is sin and the power of sin is the law.'

The darkness of death is to be found in its relation to sin and the incorrigibility of sin can only be understood in its relation to the law. These are not independent alien forces ranging against humankind. Death is the summation of all the dark consequences that flow from enmity with God. It is dealt with as that enmity is put away, not by the law which empowers sin but by the acquittal of sin that comes by grace through faith, flowing from the death of Christ. Christ's resurrection is not an expression of his own divine power. He was raised from the dead by an act of God through the Holy Spirit. This was his justification, the recognition of his life and ministry by the Father. It is an event which is to be repeated among all those who are in his fellowship. Christ's resurrection is the announcement that he has been faithful, that reconciliation has been won. It points to the efficacy of the cross in establishing peace. Through it the Holy Spirit reveals his divine sonship.

The suggestion here is that it is a mistake to think that the victory-type language used to describe the defeat of death or the putting away of sin requires a victory theory of salvation. The dramatic phraseology must not be taken to imply a deep dualism, that is, the existence of death or the law as independent realities acting as opponents of God. It is far better to recognize that this is but a triumphal or dramatic expression of the outcome of Christ's work of mediation. Victory language does not require a victory model of salvation.

What of the New Testament's testimony to Christ's destruction of the devil? Is this also to be understood in mediatorial terms? Again it is probably most helpful to examine one of the key biblical passages describing this event. 'Since the children have flesh and blood, he too shared in their humanity so that by his death he might destroy him who holds the power of death – that is, the devil – and free those who all their lives were held in slavery by their fear of death' (Heb 2. 14, 15).

A number of interesting points arise. The writer's line of argument in this chapter is that the divine Son needed to take human form to accomplish his saving ministry, which includes the destruction of the devil. This emphasis on the active humanity of Christ is an indication that we have here a mediatorial rather than victory frame of reference. But of particular interest here is the relation of the destruction of the devil with his status as the one who holds the power of death and with the consequent freedom of those enslaved by their fear of death. The devil and death are here tightly linked. But we have seen above that death is not to be considered as an independent entity opposing God and that our release from the bonds of death is the fruit of Christ's atoning work.

The two biblical narratives which historically have been understood to give the fullest account of the devil's interaction with the individual are the stories of the temptation of the primordial pair in the Garden of Eden and the temptation of Christ in the wilderness. In the Genesis story Adam failed and fell because he gave room to temptation. Christ conquered, so to speak, because he held on in faith, parried the temptations with the scriptures and refused to give ground. Paul in Ephesians 6 describes the Christian battle with principalities and powers. All he asks of the Christian is that he or she, fully protected with the armour of God, should stand firm. The devil is defeated, so to speak, when temptation is resisted. There is a tendency to view the devil as the cause of sin, but it seems equally valid to argue that he is dependent on it. With the atonement of sin and sanctification of the faithful, the devil is, as it were, like a state which has lost all its territory. The cross signals not only his defeat but his destruction.

I have argued that victory over sin, the law, and death are most naturally interpreted within a mediatorial framework, where the dualism is more apparent than real and where these entities are understood not as independent alien forces but as related consequences of our estrangement from God. Even the devil's destruction is closely linked to the end of sin and death. In short, I am suggesting that the major motifs of victory language can be explained within a mediatorial theory of salvation.

Conclusion

In conclusion, it has not been established that the mediatorial model is the normative theory of the atonement. But some preparatory work has been done in removing objections to such an argument. By illustrating how the various salvation models operate in practice as competing theories, attention has been drawn to the inherent unsuitability of the victory model as a paradigm for the soteriology of Romans. I have argued that the assertion that it can explain the process of reconciliation lacks foundation. Conversely, I have indicated how the occasional language of victory in the New Testament can often be incorporated naturally within a mediation framework. The way is thus open for us to look more closely at the claim that the mediatorial theory is the normative salvation model and to offer a provisional, highly condensed answer to the question raised at the beginning: Why did God become man? It takes the shape of a master-story, presenting in narrative form the concept that Jesus is Mediator.

> *The Son became as we are so that he might, on our behalf, make peace with God.*

This is more than an account of individual forgiveness. It summarizes God's gracious intention to reorder or reconstitute around himself the broken relationships of his suffering and alienated creation through the death of his Son and by the work of his Spirit. 'For God was pleased to have all his fullness dwell in him, and through him to reconcile to himself all things, whether things on earth or things in heaven, by making peace through his blood, shed on the cross' (Col 1. 19, 20). It points to the new realm of peace or shalom under the lordship of Jesus Christ that God constitutes through his Son's ministry. This is the kingdom which Christians are called to seek in their lives and prayers.

2

The Man and the Spirit in the Story of Salvation

A master-story

In response to what is possibly the most fundamental question of the Christian faith, 'Why did God become man?', we have offered this proposal for consideration: 'The Son became as we are so that he might, on our behalf, make peace with God.'

It is put forward not as one among many other partial perspectives, but as a master-story, a condensed narrative, intended to encapsulate the whole soteriological drama played out in the Scriptures. It suggests that a particular interpretative model of salvation, one that can be described as mediatorial, is the normative soteriological theory, able to give a coherent account of the whole range of biblical metaphors and themes which refer to salvation.

To understand what we mean here by 'master-story' it is helpful to consider the fourth-century debate over the person of Christ between the Arians and the orthodox. The Arians understood Christ to be a creature, an adopted Son, whose relation to the Father was best described in terms of conformity to the divine will. They referred to an array of Scriptural texts to support their position. Opposing these ideas the orthodox sought to defend the eternal divinity of Christ by defining the relation of the Son to the Father in terms of an identity of being or essence rather than of will. The expression 'the Word became flesh' served the orthodox cause well. It offered a conceptual basis around which their exposition of Christ's person could be developed, allowing for the possibility of Christ's eternal existence and his identity of essence with the Father, along with a genuine participation in human nature. It also provided a framework to interpret and bring into some sort of harmony other perspectives on Christ's person, suggested in the Scriptures and championed by the Arians. With this special status, it is not surprising that the phrase 'in the flesh' appeared repeatedly in the orthodox creeds and that its derived noun 'incarnation' became determinative in nearly all theological reflection on Christ's person for the next thirteen hundred years.

There is no attempt at novelty in my suggestion that the soteriological master-story should be based on the concept of Christ making peace with the Father on our behalf. It is one that has guided Western theology from Augustine, through Anselm and the Reformation, until recent times. The key role of the synonyms 'reconciliation' and 'atonement' within much past soteriological discussion are a testimony to the determinative place of the concept of peace-making in theological reflection. To speak then of a master-story is to do no more than indicate in narrative form the central concepts that shape a particular framework of thought. It is a way of presenting the key ideas that determine a theological system.

The problem is that for some the proposal that 'the Son became as we are so that he might, on our behalf, make peace with God' is no longer persuasive. One might say it is not recognized as a master-story. The redemptive action suggested in it appears to be moving in the wrong direction. It seems more appropriate to interpret Jesus' life and death in terms of God's response to the world. The death of Christ is thus recognized as an expression of God's love and concern for creaturely suffering and brokenness; as the divine way of dealing with human sinfulness; as the manifest power of God in overcoming evil, death and the demonic; as God's self-revelation; or simply as God's saving action. However, what is missing in all of these expressions is any indication that Jesus might have acted as man on our behalf towards God. One could say that in overcoming the human predicament, Christ is understood as divine agent rather than as representative of humankind.

Why is this? Why does a large section of contemporary soteriological thought[11] fail to recognize the saving significance of Jesus' ministry as a human? Before seeking to answer that question let us remind ourselves of the role that such an idea plays both in the Scriptures and the Western theological tradition.

The New Testament witness

The interpretation of the incarnate Son's atoning ministry as a 'human' act before God, on behalf of humankind, is a theme taken up by a wide range of New Testament presentations of atonement.

1. An illuminating model that Paul uses to explain the saving ministry of Christ is that of his role as the 'second Adam'. The act of disobedience of the first Adam, considered as a sort of 'federal head' of humankind, led

---

[11] There are a number of modern theologians who do emphasize the significance of Jesus' humanity in his saving ministry. James Torrance says of the atonement: 'It also means the coming of God as man, to do for us as a man what we cannot do for ourselves – to present us in himself through the eternal Spirit to the Father'. See James B. Torrance, *Worship, Community and the Triune God of Grace* (Carlisle, Paternoster Press, 1996), p. 43. Dorothee Sölle, along with those who understand Christ's redemptive action as representative, affirms the soteriological significance of Jesus' human action before God; See Dorothée Sölle, *Christ the Representative* (1967). Colin Gunton moves from the fact that Jesus acts as a man before God to a reflection on the nature of his role: 'The logic is inescapable: if Jesus is man before God, then he must be said either to *represent* us or to be *substitute* for the rest of us.' See Colin E. Gunton, *The Actuality of the Atonement* (1988), p. 61.

to universal death and condemnation. Now Christ's act of obedience has resulted in righteousness and life for many (Rom 5. 12–21). The contrast between Jesus and Adam that Paul makes here is not one between divinity and humanity, rather it is a contrast between a life of obedience and one of disobedience. Paul repeatedly compares the *one man* Jesus Christ whose action brought life with the *one man* whose sin lead to death (vv. 15, 17). Whereas the first great representative or champion of humankind failed miserably, the second has succeeded gloriously. The emphasis is on the obedience of Christ in his humanity, acting faithfully where Adam had sinned. Such obedience towards God results in both righteousness and life for the new community which he represents.

2. In the first letter to Timothy the matter of the reconciliation of God and humankind is specifically addressed. 'For there is one God and one mediator between God and men, the *man* Christ Jesus, who gave himself as a ransom for all men – the testimony given in its proper time' (1 Tim 2. 5). Salvation is recognized as coming from God who wants all humans to be saved and to come to a knowledge of the truth (v. 4), but the instrument or agent of the reconciling action is described as the 'man' Christ Jesus. The word 'man' appears to have been used specifically in this context to identify Jesus the mediator with humankind in the process of reconciliation.

3. This view of Christ in his humanity mediating between humankind and God is most carefully and systematically developed in the letter to the Hebrews. The author is concerned to clarify the person or status of Christ as the ground of his reconciling ministry. First he establishes Christ's high or divine status. 'The Son is the radiance of God's glory and the exact representation of his being, sustaining all things by his powerful word' (Heb 1. 3). He goes on to argue from a number of perspectives that Jesus is also human, like us in every way. 'Both the one who makes men holy and those who are made holy are of the same family' (2. 11). 'For we do not have a high priest who is unable to sympathise with our weaknesses, but we have one who has been tempted in every way as we are – yet without sin' (4. 15). The author believes that to demonstrate the full and complete humanity of Christ is necessary as there are aspects of the reconciliation of humankind with God, which can be accomplished only by a human. 'For this reason he had to be made like his brothers in every way, in order that he might become a merciful and faithful high priest in service to God, and that he might make atonement for the sins of the people. Because he suffered when he was tempted, he is able to help those who are being tempted' (3. 17, 18). 'Since the children have flesh and blood, he too shared in their humanity so that by his death he might destroy him who has the power of death … and free those who all their lives were held in slavery by their fear of death' (2. 14, 15). Hebrews clearly portrays Jesus as truly human, empowered by the Holy Spirit giving himself up to God. 'How much more, then, will the blood of Christ, who through the eternal Spirit, offered himself unblemished

to God ... (9. 14). The efficacy of the atonement is dependent on Christ's human action towards God.

4. The Synoptic Gospels do not expound a carefully developed soteriology but they do tell the story of the passion of Jesus at some length and in careful detail. It is everywhere apparent that their focus is not so much on the manifestation of divine power as it is on human suffering and fortitude. They suggest that a critical episode in the tragic drama of Jesus' last days was his time of agonized prayer in Gethsemane. The story as told in the Gospels implies that the trials facing Jesus centred on his experience of life as man: his faith in God, obedience to his will and openness to suffering, even in the face of his deep fears. Although not explicitly stated the emphasis is clearly on Jesus in his human weakness engulfed in deep turmoil as he seeks to know the Father's will. The words of dereliction on the cross in Matthew's account reinforce the interpretation that we have here the account of a man struggling with his God.

5. The climactic moment in the book of Revelation takes place as the author finds himself privileged to view a momentous drama unfolding before the presence of Almighty God. Around the celestial throne are the four creatures, the elders and the seven spirits. In the right hand of God there is a sealed scroll indicating his divine decrees and redemptive purposes. A mighty angel asks 'who is worthy to break the seals and open the scroll?'(Rev 5. 4). But no one appears and the author weeps as the divine will and purposes appear to be frustrated. Then one of the elders announces that there is one who is able to open the scroll 'See, the Lion of the tribe of Judah, the Root of David has triumphed' (Rev 5. 5). In the central court of heaven appears a person with a human ancestry, the Jewish definition of what it is to be truly human, who is able to unlock God's plan for eternal salvation and fulfil his redemptive purpose.

The New Testament repeatedly affirms that the atoning work of Christ is something that Jesus does as a man towards God. It is interesting that such a perspective does not appear in any way to undermine the recognition by each of its authors that salvation comes wholly from God.

The testimony of historical theology

When we turn to the soteriology of the Early Church the direction is initially somewhat different. The Early Fathers tended to interpret salvation in terms of enlightenment, immortal life and freedom from the demonic. These all flowed from the divine power manifest in Christ. Their occasional references to the themes which suggest a human action towards God, like his sacrificial death and the concepts of expiation and propitiation, have a conventional ring, suggesting that their use of them owed more to their common occurrence in the New Testament than to the integral part they played in their own theological thought.

1. Although Cyril of Jerusalem, Tertullian and Hilary of Poitiers made a beginning, it was Augustine who offered the first reflective account on the concept of sacrifice as a way of understanding the life and death of Christ. His awareness of the complexity of the issues is apparent in the following passage.

> In such wise that, whereas four things are to be considered in every sacrifice, – to whom it is offered, by whom it is offered, what is offered, from whom it is offered, – the same One and true Mediator Himself, reconciling us to God by the sacrifice of peace, might remain one with Him to whom He offered, might make those one in Himself for whom he offered, Himself might be in one both the offerer and the offering.[12]

But his most penetrating insight, it seems to me, was his appreciation that Christ's mediatorial role, through which humankind and God were to be reconciled, was accomplished in his human nature.

> For as man, he is our Mediator; but as the Word of God, he is not an intermediary between God and man because he is equal with God, and God with God, and together with him one God.[13]

2. It was some six centuries before the Western Church in the person of Anselm of Canterbury developed these ideas into a major systematic treatise. In his *Cur Deus Homo* he used the concept of satisfaction to explain what it was that Christ as man and on behalf of humankind offered as priest to God in order that there might be reconciliation and forgiveness.

The model underlying Anselm's understanding of the divine-human relation was that of a servant to his feudal lord to whom he owes satisfaction in the event of any failure to render the homage that is his due. In sinning we have defrauded and thereby dishonoured God. This creates our central problem: how shall the outstanding debt to God be paid?

> It is therefore necessary that either the honour abstracted shall be restored, or punishment shall follow; otherwise God were either unjust to Himself, or were powerless for either, which it is a shame even to imagine.[14]

The satisfaction required by God must bear a direct proportion to the sin committed, whose gravity is in turn related to the dignity of the person offended. This level of satisfaction, although required of us, lies

---

[12] Augustine, *On the Trinity*, The Nicene and Post-Nicene Fathers, (Grand Rapids, Michigan, William B. Eerdmans, 1975ff) 4.19, p. 79.

[13] Augustine, *Confessions* (London, Penguin Classics, 1977) 10.43, p. 251.

[14] Anselm, *Cur Deus Homo* (Edinburgh, John Grant, 1909), book 1.13, p. 28.

outside human possibilities. Being a payment 'which God only can, and man only should, make, it is needful that it should be made by one who is both God and man' (2. 7, p. 67).

Whether or not the concept of satisfaction in the form described above is an idea too closely linked to the world-view of medieval feudal society to be of ongoing service to the Church is not of final significance. What is important is that through it Anselm gave serious and systematic consideration to the atonement as an event accomplished by human agency that had God as its object, thereby paving the way for the major developments that took place in soteriological discussion during the Reformation, particularly in the areas of justification and forgiveness.

3. What might be considered as the passive subjection of Christ to the law and to death in the theology of Anselm is transformed by Luther into the heroic action of a mighty warrior doing battle on our behalf against all our principal enemies. Christ saves by his powerful action and ultimately by means of his divinity in overcoming sin, the law, death and the devil. There appears to me to be less emphasis in the writings of Luther that it is Christ as man that actively mediates between man and God.

Anselm and Luther illustrate two complementary strands in the soteriology of the Western tradition. These found a high level of integration in the work of John Calvin. His understanding of Christ as the God-man Mediator allowed him to bring together in his soteriology both the dramatic theme of conflict and victory won through Christ's divine power and also the idea of atonement achieved through the obedience, satisfaction and sacrifice offered by his humanity.

> ...since as God only he could not suffer, and as man only could not overcome death, he united the human nature with the divine, that he might subject the weakness of the one to death as an expiation of sin, and by the power of the other, maintaining a struggle with death, might gain us the victory.[15]

For Calvin, Christ in his humanity opposed the disobedience of man with his own obedience, satisfying the justice of God and paying the penalty of sin.

In summary, the theory that Jesus' atoning ministry is the action of one who is 'man' performed on our behalf towards God flows naturally from the biblical testimony and is in harmony with some of the most significant minds of classical Christian thought.

---

[15] John Calvin, *Institutes of Christian Religion*, trans. by Henry Beveridge (Grand Rapids, Michigan, William B. Eerdmans, 1970) II.xii.3, p. 402.

The locus of divinity

Why has much of modern soteriology abandoned this perspective? Why, when the Scriptural witness is so clear, does it no longer recognize that a vital dimension of Christ's saving ministry is that which he does in his humanity on our behalf? The answer, I suggest, is in part christological. What has become the normative understanding of the person of Christ has brought its own determining perspective to the interpretation of soteriology. It is concerned that the emphasis on the human action of Jesus outlined above is Nestorian: that it implies an unacceptable breach between the divine and the human in Christ's person. It also has difficulty allowing the sort of space between the agency of God, the Father, and that of Jesus Christ, that the human mediatorial action of Jesus towards God seems to require.

In short, to defend a mediatorial theory of the atonement one needs to consider the factors that have shaped christological development since the Enlightenment. This will then provide a better position to understand why our christology so often struggles to affirm a master-story of the form 'the Son became like us so that he might on our behalf make peace with God'?

The argument from miracles

The unsettling question that the Enlightenment posed for many areas of intellectual endeavour and in particular for that of Christian faith was one of epistemology: how can we be sure of what we know? The triumph of Newtonian physics in the seventeenth century and the widespread respect that developed for what has become known as the scientific method raised difficult questions about the basis of our knowledge in theological matters. Kepler's laws of planetary motion were recognized as being more trust-worthy than Aristotle's reflections on the motion of the celestial bodies. As the classical philosophers were shown to be quite wrong in matters of cosmology, the appeal to ancient authority on other issues no longer carried any weight. Where did this leave Christian truth? How could a religious system find rational support without recourse to ancient testimony? This question was taken up by the religious philosophers of the age who in the face of this new scepticism, published a number of apologetic treatises on the inherent reasonableness of Christianity. But what could be said of the person of Christ? What empirical evidence was there for the orthodox affirmation of his divine status? It was argued by Christian apologists that it was in his miracles that we had trustworthy external evidence for his divinity.

In the long run such arguments failed to persuade the Deist sceptics. Discussions about the miracles of Jesus moved naturally back to questions about the authority of the biblical text and the veracity of its authors at a time when such an appeal was widely discredited. David Hume argued against believing in miracles on the grounds that by definition they were unusual and that the statistical evidence was consequently against them. It was, he held, more likely that the witnesses erred than the miracle occurred. A wise person should make judgements according to the weight of evidence.[16] His argument is flawed but it reflected the rational mood of the age. Those who defended miracles seemed to be trapped in a circular argument when they sought to establish the authority of the Scriptures, either through the testimony of Jesus or through the Bible's internal witness to itself. The eighteenth-century German philosopher Gotthold Lessing reminded the intellectual world of the gulf that lay between the actual events and our own time. The persuasive power of a miracle immediately observed is quite different from the testimony of a written account read some two thousand years later.

The real problem, however, with the argument from miracles is that it fails theologically. Jesus' miracles do not establish his divinity. He performed them in the power of the Holy Spirit. Luke's account of Peter's sermon on the day of Pentecost reflects the New Testament perspective. 'Men of Israel listen to this: Jesus of Nazareth was a man accredited by God to you by miracles, wonders and signs, which God did among you through him, as you yourselves know' (Acts 2. 22). The miracles pointed to the action of God through his agent, not to the divinity of the agent. Jesus was anointed with the Holy Spirit at the time of his baptism so that he might be equipped for his public ministry. The empowerment of the Spirit in his acts of exorcism was a demonstration that the Kingdom had come. 'But if I drive out demons by the Spirit of God, then the kingdom of God has come upon you.' (Matt 12. 28.) Jesus understood his own ministry as one energized by the Spirit in fulfilment of the prophecies embodied in the servant songs in Isaiah (Luke 4. 14ff) and promised his disciples that they too would perform miraculous deeds (John 14. 12). The occurrence of a miracle clearly does not, within a New Testament world-view, establish the divinity of the agent.

There are lessons to be learnt from this episode. Flawed arguments are bad for theology. The idea that Christ's miracles establish his divinity fails to do justice to Jesus' true humanity, pushing to the periphery the reality of his life as a man empowered, comforted and guided by the Holy Spirit. Historically, a weak doctrine of the Spirit among those who saw themselves as the defenders of orthodoxy obscured the manner in which Jesus' life is a paradigm of our own and contributed to the polarization of views concerning Christ's person that developed over the next two hundred years. There were of course orthodox theologians who had argued in the seventeenth century against the idea that the miracles established Jesus' divinity, most notably John Owen, the Puritan divine. But by and large

---

[16] See section X 'Of Miracles' in David Hume, *Enquiries concerning Human Understanding and concerning the Principles of Morals,* 3rd edn (Oxford, Oxford University Press, 1978).

the apparent usefulness of the connection blinded many apologists from the clear testimony of the New Testament that it was in fact theologically wrong.

The argument from salvation

The inability to provide a persuasive epistemological basis for belief in the divinity of Christ remained a central problem for christology. In the nineteenth century Friedrich Schleiermacher, deeply sensitive to the philosophical questions of the age, constructed a brilliant theological system based around the concept of our human experience of God. In it Christ was interpreted as one whose experience of God was of such an ideal nature that it was appropriate to ascribe divine status to him.

> The Redeemer, then, is like all men in virtue of the identity of human nature, but distinguished from them all by the constant potency of His God-consciousness, which was a veritable existence of God in Him.[17]

Albrecht Ritschl interpreted the unity of Jesus with God as a complete union of the will of the man Jesus with the will of God. Both these christologies, as with liberal theology generally, were essentially Arian. However exalted the religious experiences of Jesus were considered to be, or whatever redemptive role he performed on behalf of humankind, his form of divinity was always that of a created being.

The widely influential Congregational theologian P. T. Forsyth suggested a way out of this impasse. Forsyth had studied under Ritschl and had at one time embraced the ideas of his school. He now opposed them and sought to establish a christology which was able to affirm unambiguously the uncreated divinity of Christ. Rather than the miracles, Forsyth looked to Christ's saving ministry as the epistemological foundation for his divine status. Recognizing that '(s)oteriology is the way of access to Christology'[18] he held that: 'It cannot be too often recalled that the article of Christ's deity is the theological expression of the evangelical experience of his salvation, apart from which it is little less than absurd, and no wonder it is incredible' (p. 74). It is instructive to see how Forsyth goes on to develop his argument for the divinity of Christ.

> The sinner's reconciliation with a holy God could only be effected by God ... the God who willed man's salvation must himself effect it – not accept it, and not contrive it, but effect it ... If a created being, however much of a personal splendour, was the real agent either of revelation or redemption, then grace was procured from God, and

---

[17] Schleiermacher, *The Christian Faith,* (Edinburgh, T&T Clark, 1976) p. 385.
[18] P. T. Forsyth, *The Person and Place of Jesus Christ* (London, United Reformed Church, 1999), p. 220.

not given – which is a contradiction in terms. For then the effectual thing was not done by God but by another ... If a created will effected our salvation, God's reality in it is one vast stage removed, and His sole grace impaired (pp. 85–7).

Forsyth chose his words carefully to express his pivotal idea, that is, that all saving efficacy in the ministry of Christ must be ascribed to his divinity. If salvation comes through Christ, then Christ must himself be divine. The Church's experience of salvation in Christ is thus the immediate empirical basis for its affirmation of his uncreated divinity. He defended his thesis by arguing that it is required in order to secure the freedom of God, the freedom of man, the grace of God and finally that it is a defence against the excessive religious subjectivity of the hour (p. 87).

Forsyth also recognized that there is a corollary to this theory, which has to do with divine revelation. 'For only God can reveal God' (p. 324). This was an argument later taken up by Karl Barth as he also sought a firm epistemological ground for the divinity of Christ.

> In distinction from the assertion of the divinisation of a man or the humanisation of a divine idea, the statement about Christ's deity is to be understood in the sense that he reveals His Father. But this Father of His is God. He who reveals Him, then, reveals God. But who can reveal God except God himself.[19]

Pannenberg is aware of the importance of this argument and maintains that: 'The demonstration of the connection of Jesus' divinity with the concept of revelation constitutes one of Barth's greatest theological contributions.'[20]

The wider significance then of Forsyth's theory is apparent. It meant that a way had been found to speak of Christ's divinity not in the Arian sense of the exalted status of his created being, but as the identity of his personal agency with that of God. The saving and revealing acts of Christ are the saving and revealing acts of God. Through its worship and life the Church has immediate experience of Christ's salvation and so of his uncreated divine status. The Arian christology of liberal theology was soon to give way to the neo-orthodoxy of Karl Barth and his school. Theologians found themselves no longer intellectually estranged from the ancient credal statements and were even able to bring a study of the Trinity back towards the centre of theological reflection. It is consequently quite difficult to overestimate the theological sea-change and new sense of hope that came to theological thought through the development of this simple idea that Christ's saving ministry indicates his divinity. Unlike the argument from miracles it is not open to refutation from critical historical scholarship and seems to have weathered the storms of time. It has become a foundational

---

[19] Karl Barth, *Church Dogmatics,* 2nd edn, ed. by G. W. Bromiley & T. F. Torrance (Edinburgh, T&T Clark, 1980) I.1, p. 406.

[20] Wolfhart Pannenberg, *Jesus: God and Man* (London, SCM Press, 1985), p. 130.

idea in much Christian thinking in the sense that for many it now seems obvious.

The problem is of course that it is simply not true. The saving or atoning acts of Jesus in procuring[21] salvation do not establish his divinity. Again and again the New Testament emphasizes that it is also as a man, as one of us, that Jesus is able to reconcile us to the Father. Like those who argued for Jesus' divinity from the miracles he performed, the apologists here have made a logical error. A divine outcome does not require that the instrumental agent is himself God. The action might be the work of the Holy Spirit empowering human action. Not in his performance of miracles, or atoning action, or revelation, without recourse to other considerations, do we have immediate evidence or proof of Christ's divinity.

Salvation as divine act

Two major christological streams flow out of the flawed theory that Christ's saving and revealing ministry indicate his divinity. In the one pioneered by Forsyth the personality of Christ is understood to be that of the creator himself and Jesus' human agency is effectively denied. In the other, arising from the work of Martin Kähler and coming to prominence through the German dialectic theologians Bultmann, Brunner and Barth a disjunction is made between the Christ of faith and the Jesus of history, which allows the human action of Jesus to be dismissed as religiously insignificant. These are serious charges but they constitute the heart of my argument that these dominant christological forms effectively preclude an interpretation of Christ's reconciling work as a human action on behalf of humankind towards God. Let us examine the structure of these two christological types to see if such conclusions are in fact justified.

Human agency denied

In his explication of Jesus Christ as one who is both God and man, Forsyth replaced the static classical concepts of nature or being with the dynamic ones of movement and action and focused on the concept of personality in Christ as the place of union of the divine and human movements. 'We have within this single increate person the mutual involution of two personal acts or movements supreme in spiritual being, the one distinctive of man, the other distinctive of God ...'[22] 'As the union of two wills we have in Christ the union of two moral movements or directions ...' the one he

---

[21] Jesus' divine action is however apparent in the 'administration' as opposed to the 'procurement' of salvation, most clearly manifest in his sending of his Spirit and in his saving of all those that come to him.

[22] P. T. Forsyth, *The Person and Place of Christ*, p. 343.

saw as the *kenosis* or humiliation of God, the other the *plerosis* or exaltation of man. In this way Forsyth was able to give an account of the growth in grace and understanding in the life of Jesus, who is nevertheless always the eternal Son of God. As Jesus' personal history and experience enlarged so his latent Godhead became mightier (p. 349). For Forsyth there is in Christ one personality and this is the personality of the creator himself, albeit in kenotic form embracing the conditions of a developing humanity (p. 353). There is in Christ a single energy, an involution of movements, a unity of will, which he ascribed directly to the second person of the Trinity.

Put simply, for Forsyth there is in Christ a single operating principle which is the Logos, emptied of certain aspects of his divinity so that he might conform to the conditions of a developing human person. There is then no human agency in Jesus, his actions are all those of the Logos, performed within the parameters or confines of human possibilities. It is an imaginative theory but it does not work. The concept of *kenosis* in the sense that God limits his own knowledge or power is not defensible. God is always God, he does not have peripheral attributes that can be discarded or toned down and then taken up again. Second, to be human implies the exercise of human affections, understanding and will. It includes an experience not only of the limitations of human existence such as those of knowledge and ability, but also the positive human possibilities of a dependent faith in God and of empowerment by his Spirit. Now if the principle of acting and willing in Christ is simply and immediately attributed to the divine Logos, even a 'kenoticized' Logos, the direction is from divinity *outwards* and there is no space given for active and responsive human decisions *towards* God and consequently no need in Jesus for faith or enablement by the Spirit. To effectively preclude the activity of such a mind, as Forsyth does, is to construct a Christ who is less than human, even as his theory of kenoticism suggests a divinity which is less than God.

All christologies which maintain that there is only one determinative principle (*mia energia*) in the person of Jesus Christ is that of the Logos, the Word, or the eternal Son tend to fall in the type described above and fail for the same reasons. As might be expected, it is this christological perspective which tends to view any affirmation of Jesus' human ministry incipiently Nestorian.

An insignificant human nature

The main current of neo-orthodox thought has moved in a rather different direction in dealing with the problem raised by its generating theory that all redemptive and revelatory acts of Christ indicate his divine status. It has acknowledged that the human life and actions of Jesus of Nazareth are real, but because they are redemptively irrelevant, it has sought to distinguish this life from the person of Christ who remains of ultimate significance for the faith of the Church.

To understand this development one must turn to a seminal work which appeared in the late nineteenth century, a time when many were concerned about what was perceived as the destructive work of New Testament scholarship on the historical life of Jesus Christ. In 1892 Martin Kähler published his book *The so-called Historical Jesus and the Historic Biblical Christ.* He argued that the picture of Christ derived directly or dogmatically from the Bible, in contrast to the uncertain reconstruction of his person from the critical-historical studies of the Gospels, was the proper object of the faith of the Church. The persuasiveness of his argument is not our concern here. Rather what is of interest to us is the distinction he drew incidentally between the person of Christ as the object of Christian faith and the portrayal of Jesus that came to uncertain light through the application of the standard tools of historical criticism. Although he did not deal directly with the matter of this dual perspective of Jesus Christ, the very title of the book and the apparently neat solution that his argument offered to an important theological problem contributed to the dichotomy of the historic Christ and the Jesus of history (or of the concepts of *geschichte* and *historie*) becoming axiomatic in German theological studies.

What distinction did Kähler make between the Jesus of history and the Christ of faith? It is important to recognize that the term 'historical Jesus' which began for him as a description of the failed attempts of scientific research to uncover the truth about Jesus Christ, was unconsciously transposed to mean also Jesus in his humanity, or Jesus as man. To quote Kähler: 'It is clear that the historical Jesus, as we see him in his early ministry, did not win from his disciples a faith with power to witness to him, but only a very shaky loyalty susceptible to panic and betrayal.'[23] The reality of the person described here is not denied by Kähler, rather he is considered to be ineffective spiritually and therefore insignificant to the life of the Church. In the same way Kähler who had initially described the biblical Christ as simply the Christ in whom the Church believes, also uses the term with particular reference to his divinity. 'The biblical Christ is the great vital power who has reinforced the message of the church from within ... ' (p. 104). 'For the divinity of Christ ... means for us: that by virtue of which he may become the object of faith, without this faith's coming into conflict with the First Commandment and without its leading to deification of the creature' (p. 104).

Kähler appears to be putting to his reader a nexus of straightforward choices: dogmatic theology or historical-critical studies; the canonical text of scripture or the full range of sources that shed light on the history of Jesus; the Christ in whom the Church believes or the imaginative historical person of Jesus constructed by the scholars. But by the transference of meanings indicated above the reader is faced not so much with a methodological choice as a christological perspective. The assumption

---

[23] Martin Kähler, *The so-called Historical Jesus and the Historic Biblical Christ,* trans. by Carl E. Braaten (Philadelphia, Fortress Press, 1964), p. 65.

behind Kähler's challenge is that it is possible to conceive of Jesus Christ as two rather different people. And the choice is not about which of these two perspectives or persons is real, for both of them are held to exist, but rather which of them is significant for the Christian life. The underlying thesis is that historical-critical studies are appropriate only in the case of Jesus of Nazareth and do not apply to the Christ of faith who is the true concern of the Church. There is a fatal flaw in such an argument. Jesus Christ is one person and not two. Christ, the object of Christian faith, is incarnate, he has a body and the bodily history or human story is not one that can be told in isolation from his person. The confusion or illusion in Kähler's presentation is effected when the incarnate Christ of faith is imperceptibly replaced in a docetic switch by the divine Christ, the Word of God.

How Kähler's perspective was taken up by German theology is apparent in the work of the New Testament scholar Rudolf Bultmann. For him the history of Jesus can be reduced to the simple fact of his existence, that such a man lived and died. As to Jesus' teaching Bultmann argues that '(t)he message of Jesus is a presupposition for the theology of the New Testament rather than a part of that theology itself.'[24] All religious significance is centred on the *geschichte*, the historic Christ, encountered in Christian witness and proclamation through the power of the Holy Spirit. This dichotomy between Jesus and Christ means for Bultmann that a radical critique of the historicity of the Gospel accounts of Jesus' teaching and ministry not only fails to undermine the reality of the existentially experienced Christ, but can help to ensure that such an experience is one of genuine faith rather than works. Consequently, Bultmann believes that the historical reconstructions of Jesus are theologically insignificant.

Karl Barth developed this idea in the first volume of his Church Dogmatics. His equivalent to the 'Christ of faith' is the 'Word of God', encountered by the Church as 'the Lord' in the act of revelation that occurs through the proclamation of the Church and through the Scriptures. The historical Jesus, or in Barth's language 'Jesus of Nazareth', is initially, as with Bultmann, a person in himself insignificant and historically unimpressive. 'Jesus Christ is also in fact the Rabbi of Nazareth who is hard to know historically and whose work, when He is known, might seem a little commonplace compared to more than one of the other founders of religions and even compared to some of the later representatives of His own religion' (1/1, p. 165). 'The declaration of the Son of man to be the Son of God is the significance of Jesus, and, apart from this, Jesus has no more significance or insignificance than may be attached to any man or thing or period of history in itself.'[25]

[24] Rudolf Bultmann, *Theology of the New Testament: Volume One* (London, SCM Press Ltd, 1965), p. 3.

[25] Karl Barth, *The Epistle to the Romans,* trans. from 6th edn by Edwyn C. Hoskyns (London, Oxford University Press, 1932), p. 30.

Barth reverts to a more classical exposition of Christ's person in the fourth volume of the Dogmatics and also lays stress on this particular human life as the place of divine disclosure. Yet that life in itself is always a concealing and never a revealing of God. The ongoing insignificance of Jesus' human action in Barth's theology is apparent from his lack of a doctrine of the Holy Spirit in the life of Christ. The Scriptures testify that Jesus was formed, inspired, empowered, comforted, guided and finally raised by the Holy Spirit. According to Luke, Jesus understood his own ministry in terms of the Spirit resting upon him (see Luke 4. 18). The work of the Spirit in Jesus' human life is a key to understanding his redemptive ministry. The writer to the Hebrews highlights this role of the Spirit in Christ's self-giving.

> How much more, then, will the blood of Christ, who through the eternal Spirit offered himself unblemished to God, cleanse our consciences from acts that lead to death, so that we may serve the living God! (Heb 9. 14).

As soon as the dynamic and vital place of the Spirit in the person of Christ is taken seriously, the significance of his human life before God becomes apparent. The converse is also true. The failure to recognize the religious significance of the human agency of Jesus leads to a neglect of the widespread biblical testimony to Jesus as the one anointed by the Holy Spirit.

This second christological stream is thus one in which the humanity of Jesus is acknowledged to be real and complete and can be described in terms of an historical person, Jesus of Nazareth. But apart from the 'Christ' or the 'Word' this person is religiously insignificant. This christological type accepts that Jesus of Nazareth lived and acted towards God, but will not concede that there is any salvific value to such human ministry. Reconciliation is synonymous with revelation, and revelation is an event of divine self-disclosure.

The human action of Christ

Why is the failure to affirm the reality or the significance of the human agency of Christ by these two major types of modern christology so serious an error? Why is the human story of Christ of such importance for theology?

It holds together history and theology

Kähler's disjunction of the Jesus of history from the historic Christ has not been helpful to the Christian cause. It might have allowed many theologians to pursue their areas of concern for the past hundred years untouched by the difficult questions that historical criticism raised regarding the life of Jesus, but there has been a heavy cost to pay. The failure to integrate our historical research of this man from Nazareth with our belief in a transcendent Christ effectively cuts Christian faith off from its historical basis. It is not surprising that so many historically informed observers in Western culture have struggled to take seriously the claims of a religion based on an historical personage, when the history of that person is widely held by influential theologians to be irrelevant or insignificant.

Dogmatic theology must be able to affirm unambiguously that an historical or biographical study of Jesus Christ is both possible and valuable. Within its own structure it must allow that there is a human dimension to Christ which is open to critical analysis; that Jesus' knowledge and thought-patterns were influenced by his religion, culture and prevailing historical circumstances; that he needed to hear and believe in his own particular vocation; that apart from an anointing by the Holy Spirit he was powerless to heal and cast out demons; that he prayed because he needed divine help. And the study of his life and developing understanding in the context of his background, culture, religion, call, personal faith and hope in God is intricately bound up with our interpretation of his message, his ministry and his person as the object of our faith.

N. T. Wright's book *Jesus and the Victory of God* has shown that such a study can be done and done well, and consequently is, to my mind, a profound christological contribution to Christian theology. Its underlying assumption that the human life of Jesus is of fundamental significance for both the practice and proclamation of the Christian faith is surely correct.

It is the ground of Christian anthropology

Jesus as man, filled with the Holy Spirit, is the paradigm of Christian possibilities, the historical exemplification of what it is to be truly human. It is a position I have argued elsewhere.[26] Central to the discussion is the idea that the Spirit-empowered human nature of Christ is the pattern for the renewed image of God in Christian lives. Through the sanctifying work of God we are being changed into his likeness. John Owen, who understood the significance of the argument, held that 'The great design of God in his grace is, that as we have borne the "image of the first Adam" in the depravation of our natures, so we should bear the "image of the second" in their renovation.'[27] We are not directly divinized through salvation, rather we are conformed to the image of God as manifest in the Spirit-filled humanity of Christ.

There is nothing insignificant about the human nature of Jesus. There for all to see from the crib to the cross was an historical substantiation of

[26] See Alan Spence, 'Christ's humanity and ours: John Owen' in *Persons, Divine and Human,* ed. by Christoph Schwöbel & Colin E. Gunton (Edinburgh, T&T Clark 1991).

[27] John Owen, *A Declaration of the Glorious Mystery of the Person of Christ,* vol. I of The Works of John Owen, ed. by William H. Goold (London, Banner of Truth Trust, 1965), p. 171.

true humanity, lost in the Fall but renewed in this one person, the pattern to which all the people of God through the work of the Holy Spirit will be transformed.

It is necessary for soteriology

Soteriology is a plumb line of theological adequacy, a measuring rod of 'right thought'. Apollinarianism, the most carefully developed christology of the fourth century, was discarded when it was recognized as having failed to meet the practical requirements of soteriology. For much the same reason it seems to me that any christology today which does not allow that Jesus acted redemptively as a man before God on our behalf, must also be either transformed or set aside. The human action of Jesus is significant. Although the development of christological thought in the twentieth century might have provided an effective answer to liberal Arianism, it can be seen how it has led to a deep estrangement of current soteriological reflection from its biblical roots and earlier tradition. It has failed to provide an adequate framework to interpret the atonement.

An affirmation of the human action of Christ, so necessary for any historical study of Jesus, for his role as the paradigm for all Christian living, and in particular for our understanding of the atonement, does not of itself mean falling into Nestorian error. It is the historic faith of the Church, defined at Chalcedon, that the Lord Jesus Christ is truly God and truly human. Regarding his divinity he is substantially the same as the Father without any limitation or diminution. Regarding his humanity he is as we are: eating, sleeping, thinking, dreaming, believing, deciding and acting as we do, yet without sin. He is recognized in these divine and human natures without confusion, without change, without division, without separation. The distinct characteristics of each of them, which include the manner in which they operate, are preserved as they were brought together in the one person, Jesus Christ, the incarnate Son of God (see the Definition of Chalcedon).

Conclusion

We have been considering the dynamic of Christ's atoning action. In today's unshaped world of soteriological ideas, where a lack of coherence is sometimes considered a virtue, I have put forward for consideration a classical master-story of salvation. 'The Son became as we are so that he might on our behalf make peace with God.' The implicit claim is that such a story encapsulates the essence of the Christian doctrine of reconciliation. It has been shown that the mediatorial theory of salvation which underlies such a narrative is not accepted in some sections of academic thought today and I have therefore attempted in this chapter to respond to just one of the concerns raised about its implied theology. 'Can the redemptive action of Jesus Christ be described as a human act towards God?' It has been shown from the Scriptures, supported by the tradition, that it can. The difficulty that many have in accepting this idea derives in part, I have argued, from the influence of some of the dominant christological theories of the past century. They fail to allow either for the reality or for the significance of Jesus' human action. The motivation underlying their development has been looked at and I have indicated why such christologies are inherently deficient, most notably in their inadequate doctrine of the Spirit in the life of Jesus Christ.

'What are the soteriological implications of Jesus' saving ministry as a human action towards God?' is a question still to be considered. My task here has been no more than to try and clear away some of the overgrowth so that the foundations of a biblical perspective on the atonement can be uncovered. Once their outline has been charted we will be in a far better position to envisage the shape of the completed structure.

This clearing process has exposed not only the vital role of Jesus' human action before God in effecting reconciliation but also the significance of the work of the Spirit in this redemptive ministry. It is appropriate that the provisional outline be modified accordingly.

> *The Son became as we are so that through the Spirit*
> *he might, on our behalf, make peace with God.*

3

Prayer and Propitiation

A question of agency

I have argued that there are a number of perspectives in the New Testament in which the atoning ministry of Jesus is portrayed as that of a man before God. The concepts of sacrifice, faithful obedience, priestly service, and possibly even ransom (as in the half shekel ransom price) all describe a reconciling movement in which God is the object, and Jesus as subject is considered to be like us in every way. He does not just stand in solidarity with humankind. He is one of us, sharing in both our ancestry and our experience of life with all its social and moral complexity. He is therefore well qualified to go before God on our behalf. Sometimes it is argued that he represents us and speaks for us, at others that he stands before God in our stead, dying so that we might not die. On occasion the Scriptures indicate that in his own person and action Jesus incorporates all of God's people so that his burial signals our own death and his new resurrection life becomes our life source. He is the faithful brother who makes peace, the Mediator who reconciles us to God, the pioneer who opens a path of access to the Father. 'He came and preached peace to you who were far away and peace to those who were near. For through him we both have access to the Father by the one Spirit' (Eph 2. 17, 18).

The problem with the narrative of salvation which I have been describing is not that it fails to summarize faithfully major redemptive themes in the New Testament, but rather that it appears to run counter to a rather different biblical portrayal of agency in salvation, one that interprets Christ's atoning death as a demonstration of God's generosity. 'He who did not spare his own son but gave him up for us all – how will he not also, along with him, graciously give us all things?' (Rom 8. 32). Here, God is recognised as the primary agent of salvation. He is the great and gracious lover who has sought us out for himself at great cost even while we were enemies. Our salvation flows out of his determined plan and purpose. He is subject rather than object of the atoning action, which he conceived eternally and realized in time.

How can these two quite different perspectives be held together in one coherent narrative? This seems to be an unresolved problem facing soteriology. If the logic of the first presentation is followed, God appears to stand passively and perhaps even dispassionately on the edge of the redemptive drama. He is the one whose righteous anger with human sinfulness is turned away by the faithfulness of his loving and self-sacrificing son. If the second account dominates, as it has in more recent times, all those New Testament redemptive themes which portray Jesus' death as the event which achieves our reconciliation with the Father tend to be discarded or at least overlooked. The relation of his death to the forgiveness of our sins is left without an adequate rationale. Unable to integrate these ideas many atonement theories have in practice embraced one of these narratives and neglected the other.

The Scottish theologian D. M. Baillie was aware of the apparent incompatibility of these two approaches and suggested a way of bringing them together in his book *God was in Christ*. His concern is that Christ's act of self-sacrifice should not be understood as the aversion of the wrath of an angry God.[28] He argues instead that the atonement is repeatedly interpreted by the New Testament authors as a revelation of God's love. One could say that Baillie is a strong proponent of the second story. But how does he bring the first account, the biblical narrative of Jesus' self-offering to God into some sort of conceptual harmony with this view that redemption is an act of the Father's love for the world? Baillie argues that Christ's giving of himself to die on our behalf is itself the direct action of God.

> It all takes place within the very life of God himself: for if we take the Christology of the New Testament at its highest we can only say that 'God was in Christ' in that great atoning sacrifice, and even that the priest and the victim were none other than God. (p. 188).

God is for Baillie the object of the atoning work, but he is also both the priest and the sacrifice. There is consequently no disjunction between God's gift of his Son to the world and Christ's self-offering on the cross for they are both the actions of the one God.

It is somewhat surprising that Baillie should put forward such a solution. In the early sections of his book he argued ably and very persuasively against the long tradition of docetism in the Church which neglected the active humanity of Jesus, in particular, the 'human character of our Lord's moral and religious life' (p. 14). But here, when considering the meaning of Christ's death, he reduces the sacrifice of Jesus to an act that God makes of himself to himself. This argument appears to stand far closer to the discredited theory of Modalism (sometimes nicknamed Patripassianism in the Early Church because of the suggestion that the Father suffered on the cross) than it does to the language and the theology of the Scriptures. It implies that the mental turmoil of Jesus in Gethsemane as he struggled to conform to the Father's will and his later sense of desertion by God at Golgotha are more apparent than real. The whole drama of the passion is reduced to nothing more than God dealing with himself in some interior

---

[28] D. M. Baillie, *God was in Christ: An Essay on Incarnation and Atonement* (London, Faber & Faber Ltd, 1966), see pp. 186–8.

way. Baillie's account is itself a model of docetism. The need for a real incarnation within such a theory is not clear. Further, he has removed from the story all the dynamic tension between Jesus and his Father that lies at the heart of the passion narrative. In short, Baillie's ascription to one person of both Jesus' redemptive self-giving and the Father's acceptance of this offering does not work.[29]

How do we then bring together these two quite different accounts of agency – the Father's loving gift to the world of his Son and Jesus' self-offering to God on our behalf – into one integrated narrative? Our confidence that these approaches are not mutually exclusive arises from the fact that the New Testament writers seem to have had no hesitation in affirming them both. It apparently raised no logical difficulties for them that Jesus gave himself as a sacrificial offering to God and that this death was nevertheless a demonstration of God's gracious love. It is my intention to explore the relation of these two perspectives and to consider the categories of thought which enabled the New Testament authors to hold together ideas which appear to be inimical.

The intercession of the ascended Christ

The intercessory prayer-life of the ascended Christ has played a significant role in the Church's understanding of his reconciling ministry. This was particularly true in its earliest reflections on the nature of the atonement.

1. In one of the Bible's richest passages of affirmation and assurance for the anxious Christian believer, Paul uses a number of rhetorical questions as a means of persuasion. 'Who will bring any charge against those whom God has chosen? It is God who justifies. Who is he that condemns? Christ Jesus, who died – more than that, who was raised to life – is at the right hand of God and is also interceding for us' (Rom 8. 33, 34). In the light of the saving ministry of Jesus, according to Paul, there is no reason for the Christian to doubt the security of his or her relation with God. In the first place Jesus has died and through faith in him believers are no longer condemned but freely and fully acquitted by the high judge of heaven himself. But there is a further aspect to Jesus' atoning ministry. Having risen from the dead he is at present offering prayer for the people of faith at the right hand of the Father. Jesus' ongoing ministry of intercession is considered as a further compelling argument as to how the believer is inseparably bonded to the love of Christ.

---

[29] It is worth noting that the overt biblical support for Baillie's argument is pretty well limited to one phrase: ' ... God was in Christ reconciling the world to himself ... ' (2 Cor 5. 19). But it is more natural from the context to translate this expression as ' ... God was reconciling the world to himself in Christ ... ' This is the interpretation given in most modern translations. Margaret Thrall comments in the *International Critical Commentary*: 'Even so, it is scarcely likely that Paul would have intended here to make a dogmatic statement concerning Christ's divine nature in the sense of the later credal formulations. It is not clear that any commentator of the modern period understands him in this way' (p. 433). Baillie's position does not appear to have any firm biblical support.

2. The writer to the Hebrews seeks to persuade his readers that the ministry of Jesus is more effective than that of the Levitical priesthood. One of his arguments has to do with the duration of the priestly service. 'Now there were many of those priests, since death prevented them from continuing in office; but because Jesus lives for ever he has a permanent priesthood. Therefore he is able to save completely those who come to God through him, because he always lives to intercede for them' (Heb 7. 23b–25). Jesus' saving or atoning ministry does not end with his death. But this continuation of ministry is not a repetition of his dying, for his sacrifice for sin was once for all, it is rather through his ongoing intercession. The salvation of those who come to God through him is dependent on Jesus' sustained prayer for them at the Father's right hand.

3. The author of the first epistle of John is concerned with the marks of true fellowship with God, in particular, with holiness of life, with love and with the confession of sin. To the Christian readers he makes this promise: 'My dear children, I write this to you so that you will not sin. But if anyone does sin we have one who speaks to the Father in our defence – Jesus Christ, the Righteous One. He is the atoning sacrifice for our sins ... ' (1 John 2. 1, 2a). What assurance can the Christian have in the face of the darkness and guilt of serious personal sin and the consequent sense of estrangement from God that it often brings? The answer lies in the redemptive ministry of Christ. On the one hand, he is the atoning sacrifice for sins; on the other, he is our advocate arguing our case before the Father. In short, he is praying for us.[30]

Models of intercessory prayer

We find then in these major streams of New Testament theological reflection the shared assumption that the reconciliation of the believer with God is in part dependent on the ongoing intercessory ministry of the risen and ascended Christ.[31] What are the models or paradigms that these

[30] Dorothée Sölle in her book *Christ the Representative: An Essay in Theology after the 'Death of God'* is led by her own argument to the conclusion: 'It is a vital element in Christ's existence as a person that his representation should be an unfinished and continuing relationship, and not something he exercises all at once by virtue of a distinctive super-natural quality' (p. 70).

[31] Traditional Lutheran dogmatics divided Christ's mediatorial work into two sections, satisfaction and intercession. This perspective was maintained in Reformed theology which distinguished between Christ's oblation or self-offering and his intercession (see the Westminster Shorter Catechism, question 25). James Torrance is among those who has more recently drawn our attention to the significance of Christ's intercession: 'In Jesus Christ we have someone who is praying for you. He has heard your groans and is interceding for you and with you and in you.' James B. Torrance, *Worship, Community and the Triune God of Grace* (Carlisle, Paternoster Press, 1996), p. 38. Torrance argues that there is a close relation of Christ's prayers to our own inadequate life of prayer and when he writes of Christ praying for us he means that Christ prays in our stead. We are called to participate in Christ's life of prayer and worship.

early Christian writers had before them which enabled them to conceive of the ascended Christ as one who offered prayers on their behalf in the presence of God?

1. The Gospel narratives indicate that in his earthly ministry Jesus was a man of prayer, interceding not only for himself but also for his disciples. Luke records that Jesus prayed for Peter (22. 32) and also for those who crucified him (23. 34). John gives an outline of Jesus' intercessory prayer not just for his disciples but also for the spiritual well-being and protection of future believers (17. 1–26). It would not be surprising if those who had been with Jesus expected his ministry of intercessory prayer to continue in his new resurrected life in the presence of the Father.

2. Although it was the author of the letter to the Hebrews who most systematically developed the idea of Jesus as the true high priest entering the Holy Place with his own blood, all New Testament references to Jesus' death in sacrificial terms are to be understood in the wider context of the Jewish cult and its priestly service. Among the various actions performed by the high priest in his ministry, two aspects of the atoning action are given particular significance. First, there is the death or blood-shedding of the sacrificial animal. Second, there is the entrance of the high priest with the blood-sacrifice into the presence of God. He enters as the representative of the twelve tribes of Israel, symbolized by the twelve precious stones on his breast-piece. As he stands before the mercy-seat the people of Israel are, as it were, brought before God through the priest's intercessory presence. It seems more than likely that in these actions of the high priest we find a theological paradigm by which the New Testament authors were able to interpret Christ's atoning work as including both his sacrificial death and his ongoing intercessory prayer suggested by the description of his entry into 'the Most Holy place once for all' (Heb 9. 12).

3. The Servant Song of Isaiah 53 highlights the twofold nature of the Servant's saving ministry: 'For he bore the sins of many, and made intercession for the transgressors' (Isa 53. 12c). The deep influence of this song on the soteriology of the Early Christian Church gives further indication as to why the New Testament authors were comfortable using the parallelism of sin-bearing and intercession to explain the atoning ministry of Jesus.

4. The New Testament authors were heirs to a literary tradition in which the nation's spiritual leaders were described on occasion as standing on behalf of a community under judgement and pleading with God to be merciful towards it. Abraham prayed that Sodom, the home of Lot, should be spared from divine destruction (Gen 18, 19). Again and again Moses found himself beseeching God not to destroy the faithless children of Israel. 'So Moses went back to the Lord and said. "Oh, what a great sin these people have committed! They have made themselves

gods of gold. But now please forgive their sin – but if not, then blot me out of the book you have written"' (Exod 32. 31, 32). (See also Exod 32. 11, 12; Num 11. 1, 2; 12. 13; 14. 1–23; Deut 9. 18, 19, 25, 26; 10. 10). Jeremiah remonstrates with God, 'Remember that I stood before you and spoke in their behalf to turn your wrath away from them' (Jer 18. 20b). Job was required to pray for his two friends that they might not be punished as they deserved (Job 42. 7–9). As he was being martyred Eleazar is recorded as having prayed: 'Be merciful to your people, and let our punishment suffice for them. Make my blood their purification, and take my life in exchange for theirs. (4 Macc 6. 27–9). Paul continues this pattern as he prays for the salvation of his unbelieving fellow Jews, ready to offer himself as one to be cursed and rejected by God for the sake of his people (Rom 10. 1, 9. 1–3). It was no strange thing then for the New Testament authors to position Jesus within this tradition as the one who now stands on behalf of his people, praying to God that he might be merciful and forgive them their sins.

Resurrection and intercession

The soteriological significance of the ascended Christ's intercession meant that the resurrection itself was considered as having atoning value. 'He was delivered to death for our sins and raised to life for our justification' (Rom 4. 23). As the resurrection is a logical prerequisite for Christ's ministry of prayer at the right hand of the Father, the efficacy of the latter could be attributed to the former. This dependence of the forgiveness of sins on Christ's resurrection in Paul's thought is also indicated in his extensive discussion on the future resurrection of Christians. 'For if the dead are not raised, then Christ has not been raised either. And if Christ has not been raised your faith is futile; you are still in your sins' (1 Cor 15. 16, 17). The theology of the author of Hebrews is similar, as he brings together the themes of Christ's resurrection, ascension and intercessory prayer into the single idea of Christ entering the presence of the Father in heaven. 'For Christ did not enter a man-made sanctuary that was only a copy of the true one; he entered heaven itself, now to appear for us in God's presence' (Heb 9. 24). He offers no distinct account of Christ's resurrection apart from his atoning entry into the true sanctuary in the presence of the Father. Resurrection, intercession and atonement are bound tightly together in this one concept.

Death and intercession

We see then that the New Testament writers understood the atoning action of Jesus to include not only his self-offering but also his ongoing intercessory prayer. In all the key texts referring to it, the purpose of the prayer of the ascended Christ is closely related to the saving effects of his death. His intercession and his self-sacrifice thus function somewhat like two oxen pulling together under one yoke. Although they are distinguishable they work alongside one another to achieve a common purpose or goal. What is that goal? The intercessions of Christ serve for us as a guide, revealing the categories of thought in which these authors interpreted the purpose of Christ's death. In short, prayer for divine forgiveness, for God to be merciful, is a key aspect of the conceptual framework by which they viewed the atonement. Jesus' self-offering, his giving of himself over to death, was understood by them within the general structure of his coming before God on behalf of men and women and seeking God's favour, that is, God's mercy for those who lie under divine judgement.

This understanding of Christ's death within the broader framework of seeking divine favour or mercy is reflected in three or four significant soteriological passages in which his death is explained in terms of propitiation – that which is intended to bring about God's favour. (See Rom 3. 25; 1 John 2. 2; 4. 10; and possibly Heb 2. 17.) The interpretation of these passages and in particular the precise meaning of the word-group (*hilasmos, hilasterion*), historically translated as 'propitiation', has been the focus of considerable scholarly attention this past century. The justifiable concern of many is that 'propitiation' should not be understood in the pagan sense of bribing a vindictive and vengeful deity. And it is this theological consideration that has led some scholars to seek alternative ways of translating the concept.[32] But I am suggesting that there is no need to discard completely the natural meaning of the word. Instead propitiation should be interpreted in these places broadly as that which seeks God's favour and forgiveness, in harmony with the theme of Christ's intercessory prayer. And this is by no means either a pagan or unbiblical idea. Rather, the use of propitiation in this sense serves to emphasize how closely related in New Testament thought is the efficacy of the mediatorial death of Jesus to the prayers of the risen Christ.

Agency in prayer

The aim of this chapter is to discover how the New Testament authors were able to hold together two somewhat different views of agency in the atonement: that of the Father's giving of his Son to the world, and the Son's sacrificial offering of himself to God. Now, if intercessory prayer is a significant part of the conceptual framework within which they interpreted

---

[32] C. H. Dodd's scholarly article in the *Journal of Theological Studies*, xxxii (July 1931), argues that the *hilaskomai* word group should be translated as 'expiation' rather than 'propitiation'. Leon Morris's careful study on propitiation in *The Apostolic Preaching of the Cross* (London, Tyndale Press, 1960) appears to me to have countered effectively all Dodd's main lines of argument.

Christ's death, the manner of its operation might well shed light on their understanding of agency in the atonement.

However, what is actually entailed in a prayer that God might forgive those who have sinned against him is, however, far from easy to explain. Take a fairly typical incident recorded in the book of Numbers:

> Now the people complained about their hardships in the hearing of the Lord, and when he heard them his anger was aroused. Then fire from the Lord burned among them and consumed some of the outskirts of the camp. When the people cried out to Moses, he prayed to the Lord and the fire died down (11. 1, 2).

How is this passage to be understood? On first reading it appears to be comparatively straightforward. God answers Moses' fervent prayer for the lives of those who have displeased him. But the matter becomes more complex when we consider some of its theological implications. The fire that was quenched by God is the fire of his own divine wrath against the people's faithlessness. It would seem that in answer to Moses' prayer God puts away his own anger. But this immediately raises a host of perplexing questions. Does God need to be petitioned to put away his own wrath? Is he in some sense unwilling to forgive? How is the prayer of Moses, a mere servant of God, able to turn away the divine, holy displeasure with human sinfulness? What are the implications of such an idea for God's sovereignty, his immutability, his wisdom and his goodness?

These are not problems confined to this particular Old Testament incident. They are present in all those accounts in which the nation's spiritual representatives pray that God might turn from his anger and show compassion on the faithless Hebrew community. They are also implicit in each incident in which those who have been humbled by an awareness of their wrongdoing cry out to God for mercy. A central function of the first temple, according to the account of Solomon's prayer in 1 Kings, is that it might be a place where God who dwells in heaven hears the people's cry for mercy and forgives them (8. 27–53). The New Testament *locus classicus* of such a prayer is Luke's account of the parable of the Pharisee and the tax collector who entered the temple to pray. 'But the tax collector stood at a distance. He would not even look up to heaven, but beat his breast and said, God have mercy on me a sinner' (18. 13). Now a simple cry for mercy of this form cannot be isolated theologically from a whole network of closely related concepts. It is implicitly a prayer for transgressions to be forgiven; for the decision of righteous condemnation against the sinner to be overturned; for a state of reconciliation or peace with God to replace one of enmity or hostility. Ultimately it is a prayer that God might look favourably on the sinner or, to put it negatively, that he might put away his own displeasure or anger with his or her sin. A literal translation of the Greek words used here is 'God be propitious (*hilastheti*) to me'. It suggests that God might bring an end to his anger with the tax-collector's wrongdoing. We see that the intention of the prayer of the tax collector is not so different from that of Moses described in the incident above.

The difficulties that come to light, then, in the consideration of Moses' prayer are consequently inherent in every heartfelt prayer that God might be merciful. They are embedded in the whole structure of the Church's intercessory and liturgical life. They are of course also an integral feature of Jesus' own continuing life of prayer as our advocate with the Father, arguing our case and seeking a decision in our favour. How are they to be explained? What is the causal relation between such prayer and the expression of God's favour, the experience of divine forgiveness? I am suggesting that this question sheds light not only on the efficacy of intercessory prayer but on the whole issue of agency in the atonement. How are we to respond to it?

Seeking answers

First, some would simply deny the underlying premise that God's favour needs to be sought; that to call out for divine mercy is an informed human activity. In the nineteenth century John McLeod Campbell wrote an influential book called *The Nature of the Atonement* challenging certain tenets of the Reformed soteriology which had long shaped Christian thought in Scotland. It was for him almost self-evident that the reality of God's love was not endangered by human sinfulness. 'For it ought not to be difficult to believe that, though we have sinned against God, God still regards us with a love which has survived our sins.'[33] According to him the initiating role of such love meant that divine forgiveness was in fact prior to the atoning death of Christ.

> But if God provides the atonement, then forgiveness must precede atonement; and the atonement must be the form of the manifestation of the forgiving love of God, not its cause (p. 16).

The assumption here is that God is by his nature loving and therefore favourable to us whatever we do, quite apart from the atoning work of Christ. Human sin can not threaten God's favour towards us. Whatever the argument for such a conclusion – and I believe it is flawed – the idea that the nature of God implies that we have nothing to fear from God arising out of our human sinfulness is, as I see it, a gross and dangerous presumption that is far removed from the religious world-view of either the Jews or early Christians. Let us briefly consider an aspect of each of these.

For the Jews the Exile was a critical experience that shaped both their theology and religious practice. Many have recognized that the surprising survival of both their nation and religion was due in part to the way in which the people's sufferings were interpreted by those in captivity. The writings of Jeremiah and Ezekiel along with other prophets helped the

---

[33] John McLeod Campbell, *The Nature of the Atonement and its relation to Remission of Sins and Eternal Life*, 5th edition (London, Macmillan & Co., 1878), p. 16.

Jews to understand the Exile as the outcome of God's judgement against them. The recognition that their present predicament arose out of their having offended God by their breach of his law, particularly its social requirements, opened the way for them to seek him in humble repentance and take hope in his promise that he would one day restore them to their own land. The great error of their forebears had been to presume on God's favour and protection notwithstanding their unfaithfulness. The significance of the temple in Jerusalem as the place where the divine glory was manifest gave an earlier generation false hope that God would never allow the city to be destroyed. Through the devastation that occurred in the sacking of Jerusalem and the deportation of its people the Jews learnt to their cost that the divine favour can not be assumed in the context of rampant sin.

In the New Testament the proclamation of peace with God or divine forgiveness is always linked with faith and is considered as an outcome of the work of Christ. It is never a promise that can be simply deduced from God's loving nature. Further, the doctrine of a final judgement, particularly in the teaching and parables of Jesus, but also in the writings of most New Testament authors, undermines any over-hasty assumption that God's favour can be relied on in the face of gross unfaithfulness even for those who participate in the sacramental life of the church (see 1 Cor 10. 1–13).

Campbell's argument that God's forgiveness precedes the atonement rests on his understanding of divine forgiveness as meaning much the same as the love of God. He writes: 'Forgiveness – that is, love to an enemy surviving his enmity, and which, notwithstanding his enmity, can act towards him for his good; this we must be able to believe to be in God towards us, in order that we may be able to believe in the atonement' (p. 15). He is of course right that the atonement flows out of God's loving initiative. But he is quite wrong to make a simple identification of love and forgiveness. The wonder of God's love is that he loved us *while* we were still his enemies, that is, while we were estranged (see Rom 5. 8). Forgiveness has to do with a putting away of that enmity, the remission of guilt. Love initiates a process that results in forgiveness and reconciliation. One could say that we are forgiven *because* we are loved, but the beginning must not be confused with the end.

Campbell's soteriology is of course far richer than the discussion above might suggest. His theory of atonement is essentially mediatorial, emphasizing the role of Christ in his humanity acting on behalf of humankind confessing to God the sin of men and women. Sometimes he speaks in a language that appears to oppose radically the direction of the argument just quoted.

> We do not understand the divine wrath against sin, unless such confession of its evil as we are now contemplating is felt to be the true and right meeting of that wrath on the part of humanity. We do not understand the forgiveness that is in God, unless such intercession as we are now contemplating is felt to be that which will lay hold of that forgiveness and draw it forth (p. 128).

Nevertheless his earlier unguarded advocacy of a position that has since become widely popular, that divine forgiveness can be assumed quite apart from the atonement, is one that it is important to rebut.

A more constructive way of solving the problems inhering in the 'petition for mercy' is to argue that our prayers are effective in so far as they are in harmony with God's own intention or purpose. We do not bend the divine will in our prayers, rather we conform to it. We are, through our prayers, brought into harmony with what God is doing. There is strong biblical support for the idea that we are called to pray in accordance with the will of God. Jesus himself in Gethsemane ultimately submitted himself in his prayers to what he understood to be the will of his Father. Where the intention of God is unclear it is argued that the Holy Spirit has been given to guide or direct the prayers of the faithful so that they might pray as they ought. More than that, our prayers can be understood as the Holy Spirit interceding with the Father through us. Now if through the work of the Spirit our prayers are in accord with the divine purpose, then the sovereignty, immutability and goodness of God are not threatened by a doctrine of prayer, even if it be the prayer that God might no longer be angry with our sin.

The difficulty with such an interpretation of prayer, as it stands, is that it implies that our intercessions are somewhat pointless. They are not unlike the cartoon of the rooster who rises before dawn and then dramatically directs the sun up over the horizon. He might feel very satisfied with his morning's work, but we have a strong suspicion that the sun would have risen without him. Are our prayers no more than a shadowing of God's intentions and actions, a reflecting of what he was going to do anyway? Is their value entirely subjective? Do they have no influence on an external reality? If they do not, how can Jesus' prayers at the right hand of the Father bring any comfort or assurance to the believer? How can they be an effective part of his atoning action?

It seems to me that if prayer is not to be an empty charade, we are compelled to recognize that it is in 'some sense' effective in achieving that for which it petitions. But the critical question appears again: how or in what sense are prayers effective? What is the causal relation between our prayers and the manifestation of divine favour and forgiveness? To clarify the question it might be of value to reflect for a moment on the subject of efficacy or cause.

Different types of cause

Even without any training as logicians, we are generally aware that there are a number of quite different sorts of answer that might be given to explain the occurrence of a particular event. The context of the question normally determines the type of answer that is expected. For instance, with just a little help from Aristotle and scholastic theology,[34] we might reply to the question 'Why is the light on?' in at least four quite different ways:

1. 'Because it is too dark for me to read without it.' Although we would normally think of this as the purpose of the light being on, it is not too difficult to see why it was once described as the final cause.
2. Because I turned it on. The suggestion here is that the light shining flows from my personal decision and consequent action. We might say that I am the primary agent, the first cause.
3. Because the flow of electricity from the power supply is heating the filament in the light bulb. This is how we might respond to someone seeking a scientific explanation of the shining light. Although it is not quite how Aristotle used the term let us refer to this type of explanation as the material cause.
4. Because the light switch is in the 'on' position. This answer is both similar and yet a little different to the one above. The switch being 'on' is one of a chain of realities necessary for the light to be shining. I think it can be helpfully described as an instrumental cause along with a whole host of other necessary conditions such as the proper state of the wiring, the condition of the filament in the bulb, and the electricity bill having been paid.

Now this analysis of the various types of cause behind this particular occurrence is of course somewhat arbitrary and imprecise and there is no certainty that it can be applied meaningfully to quite different sorts of events. Its general value, however, is that it reminds us that in most situations there are certain explanations of cause or agency that by no means exclude others. Sometimes they are simply different answers given to subtly different questions. Let us tentatively consider how the application of this form of analysis can be of help when we consider the matter of the atonement and the part played by prayer in effecting reconciliation and the forgiveness of sins.

First, I have argued that the immediate purpose of the atonement is to achieve peace with God. Of course the divine intention is far more than this. Within the reconciled community the Holy Spirit is given to restore the divine image as it inheres in Jesus and so manifest the nature of God in this world, bringing glory to his name. This, or some related outcome, is what the atonement seeks to achieve ultimately. It is, we might say, the final cause.

Second, God is recognized as the true source of salvation. Reconciliation is from first to last a free act of his grace. He is the primary or first cause of the atonement. Atonement is his plan. It derives from his loving intention.

---

[34] A similar division of the various types of cause that I will develop is apparent in the Council of Trent's discussion on Justification. 'The causes of this justification are: the final cause is the glory of God and of Christ and life everlasting; the efficient cause is the merciful God who washes and sanctifies gratuitously, signing and anointing with the holy Spirit of promise, who is the pledge of our inheritance, the meritorious cause is His most beloved only begotten, our Lord Jesus Christ ... '(Chapter VII of the Decree concerning Reform, the Sixth Session.)

What within this analysis can we say of prayer? It seems to me helpful to describe prayer as 'instrumental' in salvation. Although God is complete and sufficient in himself, he has freely chosen to use the agency of his creation, that which is other than himself, to accomplish his purpose, to bring glory to his name. He uses the Church's newly formed characteristics of love and compassion to minister to the suffering of a world in pain. He speaks through the words of human proclamation to invite the careless and the weary to respond to his grace. In particular, he uses the prayers of the humble and pre-eminently those of his ascended Son as his instruments to effect reconciliation. The fact that God uses such tools or agents to accomplish his purposes in no way undermines his sovereignty or his freedom. He remains the first cause.

We are able to affirm then that appropriate prayer is that which is done through the Spirit in accordance with the divine will. But this does not mean that prayer is an empty echoing of God's actions. It is in itself an effective instrument in achieving the divine purpose. By God's grace it can be a channel to bring about that for which it petitions. Prayer along with other human responses to God's good news, including faith and repentance, are together part of what can be described as the 'instrumental cause' of reconciliation. They are significant, they are necessary for salvation, but, and this is of the utmost importance, in New Testament thought no credit or merit is attributed to them. Their whole nature is to look away from themselves towards God's provision. The relation between what I have described as the primary and instrumental causes in an analysis of salvation is apparent in the letter to the Ephesians.

> For it is by grace you have been saved, through faith – and this is not from yourselves, it is the gift of God – not by works so that no one can boast. (Eph 2. 8, 9).

God's grace, his disposition to be merciful, is the primary cause of salvation. Faith, the appropriate response to the gospel, although instrumental in salvation and therefore necessary, can take no credit. There is no merit in it. It provides no basis for a boastful attitude. It is a God-given gift through which salvation is received. The prayer for mercy, the call to God that he might be favourable, appears to fit into this pattern, operating in the same manner as faith. We are encouraged to respond in this way to the Gospel. 'Everyone who calls on the name of the Lord will be saved' (Rom 10. 13).

It makes sense then to recognize that the prayer for mercy is an instrument used by God to reverse his judgement against sin, and forgive the penitent. God is the primary agent in all prayer. He is both its true source and the one who freely responds to its appropriate requests. It is out of his love and grace that sin is forgiven. But this is not to deny the significance of the one praying or the propitiatory effectiveness of the prayers offered. Through the enabling of God's Spirit the work of the human intercessor is both real, effective and, in so far as he has appointed it, necessary as an instrument in salvation.

He will provide the lamb

What of the death of Christ? How are we to understand its causal role in effecting reconciliation, in procuring forgiveness? Our concern at this point is not to offer an explanation of why it is efficacious, but rather to discern what place it occupies in the causal framework of New Testament soteriology.

I have argued that the New Testament authors interpreted the significance of Christ's intercessory prayer as being closely associated with the efficacy of his death, sharing with it the same immediate goal, that is, the procurement of peace with God, the realization of divine favour and forgiveness. They affirm uniformly that God in his grace and love is the primary or formal cause of this reconciliation or salvation; the single source of the stream from which all of its spiritual blessings flow. But it is the death of Christ which is repeatedly referred to as the means by which that peace is brought about; as that which effectively deals with the problem of sin. I am suggesting that in their scheme of thought Christ's self-offering functions as the material cause of the atonement.

What is meant in the context of New Testament biblical soteriology by the concept 'material cause'? There is in the Judaeo-Christian tradition a recurring indication that God manifests his mercy and favour in response to some material reality or ritual that he has provided or instituted. Somewhat surprisingly we discover that after the flood the rainbow is given as a sign by God so that when *he* sees it he will remember his covenant and not again destroy a rebellious world by flood (Gen 9. 16). God dramatically leads the Hebrew people out of Egypt but only after he has instructed them how to slaughter and eat the Passover lamb so that when *he* sees its blood on the door posts of their homes he will spare the first-born of their sons from death (Exod 12. 23). Yahweh covenants to be God to the people of Israel but he provides a Day of Atonement so that, by his institution through priest, sacrifice and scapegoat, he might not be alienated from them on account of their sins (Lev 16. 30). Central to the whole enactment of the ritual on that day is the instruction that the goats, the blood of the bull and the burning coals are brought by the High Priest before the Lord into his presence. The idea is that God sees these things and forgives. In fact the whole Jewish cult including its worship, offerings of thanksgiving, intercession and in particular the daily sacrificial offerings for the remission of sin find their focus on the temple in Jerusalem, for that is the place God is considered to dwell. They must be done in his presence. In all of these accounts there is no suggestion that humans have discovered some method or artefact which can be used by them to placate a vengeful and recalcitrant deity.[35] On the

---

[35] Thomas F. Torrance has a very clear grasp of this idea. 'Not only the general pattern of the cult but the details of the liturgy were clearly designed to bring home to the people of Israel that they were not to appear before the Face of God with offerings embodying their own self-expression or representing their own naturalistic desires ... Thus no unprescribed oblation, no uncovenanted offering, no strange fire, no incense of their own recipe, and no ritual of their own inventing, were to be intruded into their worship of God.' *The Mediation of Christ*, rev. edn (Edinburgh, T&T Clark, Edinburgh, 1992), p. 74.

contrary the material cause is always God's institution or gift. He both gives it and then responds to it. He sees the lamb that he has provided and then responds with forgiveness and divine favour.

It is legitimate to ask 'How could these things possibly have dealt with the pollution of sin and the consequent alienation from God?' The author of Hebrews provides an unambiguous answer: ' ... it is impossible for the blood of bulls and goats to take away sin' (Heb 10. 4). He recognizes all of these things to be mere shadows, suggestive of or sacramentally pointing to the one reality which could transform the human predicament, the self-sacrifice of Christ. But these rituals do indicate a scheme of thought in which it is naturally assumed that God forgives and manifests his favour in response to some material cause which he has instituted. Ultimately the writer of Hebrews argues that there is only one such material cause, in which all the Old Testament examples participate as ancient witnesses to its future reality, and that is the death or blood of Christ, carried, so to speak, by the ascended Jesus into the presence of God.

Paul as part of his precise and careful explanation of justification says of Jesus' reconciling work: 'God presented him as a sacrifice of atonement, through faith in his blood' (Rom 3. 23). The alternative reading offered by the NIV is 'God presented him as the one who would turn aside his wrath, taking away sin.' As I have argued before, there is nothing startling or new about the idea of propitiation here. It is consistent with the whole direction of God's forgiving action in the Scriptures. God himself is the source of atoning action and as such supplies its material cause, that which brings about his favour and forgiveness. But, and this is of vital significance in understanding the nature of his love, this material cause is his own Son.

Conclusion

Why did the New Testament writers have no difficulty in speaking of the death of Jesus as both the generous gift of God to the world and the mediatorial action of Christ towards God on our behalf? To understand more clearly the categories which shaped their interpretation of the atonement I have looked briefly at the role played in their thought by the intercession of the ascended Christ. The Son's prayers for the Father to show mercy and kindness to his children are closely related in their understanding to the purpose of Christ's death. Both are propitiatory in nature in that they seek God's favour and forgiveness.

Further, I have indicated how the New Testament authors inhabited a world of thought in which the role of God as the primary source of atonement was considered to be wholly consistent with his provision of some agency which brought about reconciliation. It was a way of thinking which recognized that God provided the means which would secure his own forgiveness and favour. He would, so to speak, provide the lamb. We have seen how this perspective was developed and shaped in the Old

Testament witness to God's acts of salvation. It was a concept that was to become central in New Testament soteriological thought. God in love gave his Son so that those who believed might not perish under his righteous judgement. The nature of that gift is not so much a material object, that is, the physical blood of Jesus, but a person with his own particular narrative. It is the story of one who left his place of glory and became as we are; who learnt obedience through his suffering; and who out of zeal for his Father's glory and love for his brothers and sisters freely surrendered his life on their behalf to make peace with God. The Father's gift is nothing less than this mission of his only Son, whom he gave to the world or sent into the world empowered by his Spirit. The story of the Father's gift and the story of the Son's loving obedience thus form a single coherent narrative.

Many who hold to what might be called an exemplarist view of the atonement quite rightly discern in the cross a demonstration of the gracious love of God for the world. One difficulty that they have with mediatorial interpretations of reconciliation is that they seem to undermine God's role as the loving, primary agent of salvation. The idea that Christ has come to make peace with God suggests to them that the gracious action in this scheme of redemption is that of the self-sacrifice of Christ and that the Father's role is largely passive. He is merely the one whose anger is averted or to whom satisfaction is made. Such a concern has led to the rejection or neglect by many of mediatorial ideas of atonement notwithstanding their central place in New Testament thought.

I have argued in this chapter that God's loving gift of his Son and Jesus' propitiatory death are not mutually exclusive stories, but actually require one another and are to be held together in one redemptive narrative. I doubt if this integrated understanding of agency in the atonement can be summarized more succinctly than it is in the first epistle of John.

> This is love: not that we loved God, but that he loved us and sent his Son as the one who would turn aside his wrath taking away our sins (1 John 4. 10 NIV alternative reading).

Or with a greater sense of religious awe and wonder than is reflected in the praise song of Isaiah:

> I will praise you, O Lord.
> Although you were angry with me,
> your anger has turned away
> and you have comforted me.
> Surely God is my salvation;
> I will trust and not be afraid (Isa 12: 1b. 2a).

We see then that a mediatorial understanding of the death of Christ is able to affirm God's saving generosity in the gift of his Son to a world that he loves. The way in which the Church has sought to give theological expression to this mediation of Christ between humankind and God will be considered in the following chapter.

4

Justification as the Syntax of Redemptive Ideas

Historically, it is the idea of justification that has received greatest recognition and development by the Church as a way of interpreting Christ's mediatorial work.

The Joint Declaration on Justification

In 1997 the Lutheran World Federation and the Roman Catholic Church published a document entitled the *Joint Declaration on the Doctrine of Justification*. It was the distilled product of years of study and discussion by some of the ablest biblical, historical and theological scholars of the two communions. After vigorous open debate the declaration was solemnly ratified at the highest level of both Churches in 1999. The position of the two communions is by no means identical but there is incorporated in the document a substantial, commonly agreed, statement of belief on justification. Article 15 of the document gives some indication of the level of convergence between the two bodies.

> In faith we together hold the conviction that justification is the work of the triune God. The Father sent his Son into the world to save sinners. The foundation and presupposition of justification is the incarnation, death, and resurrection of Christ. Justification thus means that Christ himself is our righteousness, in which we share through the Holy Spirit in accord with the will of the Father. Together we confess: By grace alone, in faith in Christ's saving work and not because of any merit on our part, we are accepted by God and receive the Holy Spirit, who renews our hearts while equipping and calling us to good works.

Although we do not have here a resolution of all points of dispute between Lutherans and Catholics – for instance, it is not specified whether sanctification is an aspect of justification or a distinct work of the Holy Spirit – nevertheless, we find in the document an articulate presentation of 'justification by faith' which includes much that both communities wish to affirm concerning the doctrine. Through Christ's saving work we are accepted by God. He is the mediator of our peace with the Father.

One outcome of the discussion is the formal announcement that the ancient anathemas pronounced against one another no longer apply to the dialogue partner's position on the doctrine in so far as it is reflected in

the declaration. The ecumenical implications of such a level of consensus
are of course enormous. It is well to remember that the doctrine of 'justification by faith alone' was the principal theological issue behind the
most significant breach in the Christian Church since the Orthodox and
Catholic communions formally divided over the *filioque* clause in 1054.
Of course there were serious ecclesiological concerns that Lutherans had
with the Roman Catholic Church in the sixteenth century, but the matter
of soteriology was central. Alister E. McGrath illustrates this point with
an interesting historical detail: 'The priority of his [Luther's] soteriology
over his ecclesiology is particularly evident in his remarkable statement of
1535, to the effect that he will concede the Pope his authority if the latter
concedes the free justification of sinners in Christ.'[36] After the anathemas,
wars and schism that followed Luther's initial confrontation with the papacy,
it is remarkable that Lutherans and Catholics should now be able to reach
this level of convergence over the principal doctrine of dispute. It certainly
offers promise for future healing in a divided Christian community.

But does such a document have any theological significance? Does it
bring any clarity to our understanding of justification today, particularly
to those who don't happen to be members of the Catholic or Lutheran
communions? It would seem that many theologians and biblical scholars,
particularly in the English-speaking academy, are somewhat bemused by
the energy that has been put into this project and would reckon its significance to be more ecclesiological than theological. In some respects the
whole discussion appears anachronistic. A number of shifts have taken
place in modern times in the way the atonement is viewed, or Paul is
understood, which distances many from the soteriological concerns of the
sixteenth century. Let us consider briefly two of the movements or changes
that have taken place in more recent theological thought.

Relativism

First, it is no longer taken for granted that it is proper for the Church to
attempt to make a clear and coherent formulation of the atonement that
has abiding value for the faithful. F. W. Dillistone in his book *The Christian
Understanding of the Atonement* catches something of the mood of the age.
He argues that there are a number of different ways of interpreting Christ's
redemptive work:

> But if there are varying theological formulations of atonement in the
> New Testament how much more is this the case in later periods of
> the history of the Church. One attempt after another has been made
> to show that the death and resurrection of Jesus gains meaning and

---

[36] Alister E. McGrath *Justitia Dei: A History of the Christian Doctrine of Justification*, 2nd
edn (Cambridge, Cambridge University Press, 1998), p. 197.

power when set within a particular framework of human experience which is already reasonably familiar. How then can we decide upon the relative value of these different theories?[37]

In the world of diverse soteriological ideas, this he recognizes as the critical question: how do we judge the merit of a particular interpretation of Jesus' death? Dillistone suggests that there is no general agreement about which atonement theory is most prominent in the New Testament and even if there were that does not mean it should of necessity be so in another age (p. 26). Rather ' ... the sociological and psychological needs of a particular era will manifest themselves in such a way that a particular theory or explanation will commend itself as most relevant and meaningful at that particular time ... it does mean that no absolute sanction can be accorded to any human formulation and that every Christian theologian must be constantly seeking to relate himself imaginatively to the particular needs of his own age' (p. 26).

In his view the theologian's task is not to formulate a comprehensive abiding doctrine of the atonement but to try and discover which theory of salvation works best at a given time in a particular community. The quest for theological truth has subtly shifted to the search for religious relevance. We are no longer seeking to understand the logic or meaning of the atonement or to resolve earlier disputes, our concern is more about finding the appropriate thought patterns to express God's saving work in the modern world. The relativistic approach suggested here is guided in part by a fear of the tyranny of dogma. Dillistone describes his own position: 'This may be an empirical solution but it is the only alternative to accepting a formulation imposed by authoritative decree' (p. 26). He is unlikely to have been an ardent supporter of the *Joint Declaration*.

One immediate problem arising from Dillistone's argument, particularly for those who subscribe to broadly orthodox Christian beliefs, is 'what is to be made of other dogmas like that of the Trinity or the person of Christ?' Is their value also to be determined by how well they are received in various cultures? How we express such concepts might be shaped by society and the prevailing world-view, but the underlying dogma, for instance that God is in his being triune, is surely a reality that does not change because a particular community might be averse to such a way of thought. The question remains: 'Is there no *abiding* essence or substance to the atonement, something that the Church should seek to explicate, albeit imperfectly, for the encouragement of all the faithful and the defence of the gospel?'

The relativistic view of Christ's redemptive work suggested above is founded in part on the recognition that among the New Testament authors a number of different soteriological characteristics, models or metaphors

---

[37] F. W. Dillistone, *The Christian Understanding of the Atonement* (London, SCM Press Ltd, 1984), pp. 25, 26.

are used. It has become common practice in books on the atonement to catalogue these in terms such as sacrifice, ransom, justification, acquittal, propitiation or expiation, the defeat of evil, the overcoming of sin and participation in Christ. Depending on the scholar's preference a number of these types are expounded, developed and related to current ways of understanding, using the range of academic tools available. Such a methodology inevitably presents to the reader an array of apparently distinct soteriological types. The conclusion is natural. The New Testament authors worked with a variety of independent salvation models. A relativistic approach to soteriology appears to have been present in the Church from the very beginning. Dillistone illustrates this way of understanding:

> I have already implied that more than one theoretical framework is to be found in the New Testament itself. It would be sufficient to give a brief description of the backgrounds of the words Redemption, Justification and Propitiation to show that such is the case (p. 25).

The argument is a model of simplicity. All we have to do is look at the background to these 'soteriological' words and the diversity of atonement theories will be clearly established. The fatal, but apparently unnoticed, flaw in such reasoning is that Paul uses all three of these concepts in two consecutive verses at the core of one carefully constructed soteriological proposal.

> ... [they] are justified freely by his grace through the redemption that came by Christ Jesus. God presented him as a sacrifice of atonement [propitiation], through faith in his blood (Rom 3. 24, 25).

These supposedly independent ideas are here brought together by Paul in one extensive and considered explication of God's saving action. To understand the meaning of the atonement in the New Testament we must seek to discover how the authors, who used these concepts, related them to one another. We need, so to speak, to study their syntax, how the words work together, and not just what they mean in isolation. This is a project we will return to later in the chapter.

The place of justification in Paul's thought

Second, it is no longer generally assumed that justification is the central or dominant soteriological concept. In each of the confessions or statements of faith drawn up by the various churches during the Reformation debate, from the Formula of Concord to the decrees of the Council of Trent, justification by faith was treated as the key soteriological idea and explicated accordingly. Such a view of its central position is, however, questioned by many today.

E. P. Sanders through his book *Paul and Palestinian Judaism* has done as much as anyone to bring about this shift in perception in the English-speaking world of theology. His chapter on Paul, which is largely independent of his comprehensive study on Palestinian Judaism in the earlier sections of the book, is full of suggestive ideas that make fascinating and sometimes unsettling reading for any who have fixed or strong views on the subject. One of his major conclusions has to do with the place of justification in Paul's thought:

> There should, however, be no doubt as to where the heart of Paul's theology lies. He is not primarily concerned with juristic categories, although he works with them. The real bite of his theology lies in the participatory categories, even though he himself did not distinguish them this way.[38]

The whole network of ideas related to justification, including righteousness, judgement and forgiveness are thus seen as secondary to those of being in Christ, being members of his body, dying to sin by participation in his death and sharing in his Spirit. In the terminology of the Reformation debate one might say he believes that Paul is more concerned about sanctification than justification. But on what grounds does he make such an assessment?

Consider for a moment the general assumption that he is countering. It was widely held that what Christ achieves for our salvation corresponds in some measure to the nature of the human predicament. Our assessment of the human condition was thus seen as playing a significant part in shaping our understanding of the atonement. Bultmann reflects this perspective: 'Indeed the view that all men are sinners, which [Paul] develops at length in Rom. 1. 18–3. 20, is a basic one for his doctrine of salvation ... '[39] (p. 227). As all of humanity on account of culpable transgression lies under the righteous judgement of God, divine acquittal or the justification of the sinner is held to be at the very centre of his interpretation of God's saving work in Christ.

To challenge these conclusions Sanders finds it necessary to undermine the methodological direction outlined above. His intriguing suggestion is that Paul moves from solution to plight rather than the other way around.

> Although it would be expected in advance that the conception of the plight should precede the conception of the solution, Paul's thought seems to have run the other way (p. 475). Man's plight is basically to be understood as the antithesis to the solution to it as Paul understood that solution (p. 497).

He offers three arguments for this theory. The first is that Paul's own conversion experience moved from solution to plight: 'There is no need to

[38] E. P. Sanders, *Paul and Palestinian Judaism* (Minneapolis, Fortress Press, 1977), p. 502.

[39] Rudolf Bultmann, *Theology of the New Testament*, vol. 1 (London, SCM Press Ltd, 1965), p. 227.

think that Paul felt the need of a universal saviour prior to his conviction
that Jesus was such' (p. 443). The second is that Paul's preaching did not
begin with the human predicament: 'This means that the way the problem
is posed in Romans may not reflect Paul's actual missionary preaching. It
seems unlikely that he followed the modern fundamentalist tactic of first
convincing people that they were sinners and in need of salvation' (p. 444).
The third is that when Paul refers to the gospel it is always the solution
rather than the human condition which is referred to: 'But it is noteworthy
that he never specifies the plight of man as what is preached. It is always the
action of God in Christ' (p. 444).

Such a procedure turns a number of traditional perspectives on their
heads. We learn that the law as a way of salvation is problematic, not so
much because humans fail to fulfil its rigorous demands, but because it
would imply that there could be no common salvation for both Jews and
Gentiles – a solution to which Paul is already committed. 'Here we see
clearly the thrust that there must be one ground of salvation in order that
Jews and Gentiles may equally have access to salvation. This is, in effect,
an argument against the law as being in any way necessary for salvation'
(p. 489).

Sanders's argument that Paul moved from solution to plight in his explication of the atonement, is vital to his thesis that the heart of Paul's theology
lay not in a doctrine of justification but in participationist categories. How
do we respond to this? Sanders's presentation appears to me to be somewhat
like that of an archaeologist expounding a theory that the Egyptian pyramids
were built with the apex on the ground supporting a square base hundreds
of feet higher up. It initially seems an odd or illogical supposition, but much
that is true in life appears a little odd at first, so for a time we put aside our
incredulity and try to follow the logic of the argument. The points made in
support of the case for inverted pyramids have varying degrees of plausibility
and we wonder whether cumulatively they might indeed be worth taking
seriously. But then we notice on the lecture programme a recent photo-
graph of the Great Pyramid standing in all its glory in the Egyptian desert
with its base firmly on the ground supporting a tapering structure. The
case for upside-down pyramids immediately collapses. Sanders's argument
unaccountably does not take serious consideration of the major text
before him. In Romans, Paul has carefully built an extensive soteriological
substructure and it moves logically from predicament to solution. There is
no need to speculate about Paul's preaching, his religious conversion or the
epistemic priority of solution over plight in his own thought life. His methodology when it comes to formally explaining the atonement is quite plain and
we cannot with integrity simply turn it on its head if we want to understand
him. Logical priority is given to the human plight and the work of Christ is
God's gracious and overwhelming response to that predicament.

Without the controlling function provided by a textually informed
doctrine of the human predicament, Sanders's argument for the centrality

of participationist categories in Paul's soteriology fails, for it is inevitably circular. In his own words:

> The real plight of man as Paul learned it not from experience, nor from observation, nor from an analysis of the result of human effort, but from the conviction that Christ came to be lord of all, was that men were under a different lordship (p. 500). Thus the *purpose* of Christ's death was not simply to provide expiation, but that he might become Lord and thus save those who belong to him and are 'in' him (p. 465).

We know that Christ came to be lord of all; we infer from this that the central human predicament has to do with being under the foreign lordship of sin; the argument here is that categories of participation through which the lordship of Christ is realized form Paul's dominant soteriological theme. The circle is complete.

The human predicament

A sounder way to approach soteriology is to give due consideration to the nature of the human condition, recognizing that theories of salvation are inevitably shaped by an understanding of the plight facing us.

It is apparent that all the soteriological motifs used in the New Testament are a response to some expressed or tacit understanding of human predicament: ransom or redemption suggests prior bondage or servitude; salvation presupposes impending peril or catastrophe; reconciliation and atonement indicate that broken relationships need healing; sacrifice is related to past sins in need of expiation; justification and forgiveness are the divine responses to a condition of condemnation and guilt. Those following Sanders's approach might argue that at least the announcement of the lordship of Christ is not shaped by the nature of our predicament. But it seems to me that such a proclamation is at best ambiguous good news and although a central theme in the Christian faith, it is not, properly speaking, a summary of the gospel. This is a subject which shall be considered more fully in later chapters.

How would the human plight be described today? A multitude of apparently unrelated answers might be given to such a question, depending on who was being asked. For many it might be expressed as the lack of food for their children or fresh water to drink, or more abstractly as the dehumanizing consequences of unremitting poverty. For others it is the experience of injustice or oppression or exclusion from the life and decisions of the community. For some it is the absence of purpose or meaning as they find themselves trapped in an apparently pointless existence in the midst of plenty. Some feel estranged from love or truth or the sense of the divine. Others cry out for no more than the restoration of their health. There are those who fear death; there are those overwrought by their own addictions and propensity to do evil; there are those who are racked with guilt and shame for their past actions. For some our plight has to do with our personal angst or our sense of insignificance. One wonders if there is any sense in which we all, diverse as we are, share together in a common predicament.

Historically the Church has offered a wide range of interpretations of the nature of the human condition. In the early second-century writings of the Didache and 1 Clement it was the themes of human mortality and ignorance that were most emphasized. Although the concept of sin was certainly present in the Apostolic Fathers it was not central. Later, Justin developed the concept of free will and the consequent responsibility or accountability that humans bear for their actions even though he also believed that these are often instigated by malign demons. Irenaeus argued that Adam as primal man was a moral and intellectual child who fell easy prey to Satan, disobeying God and so losing the divine image and likeness. All men and women have participated in his deed and so share both his guilt and bondage to the devil. In the third century Tertullian, a dominant influence in Western theology, held that all souls were seminally present in Adam and from this formed an early doctrine of original sin. He argued that although humans have free wills they are, nevertheless, biased towards sin from birth and are in need of illumination and instruction. These ideas were later developed in the wider Church, particularly by Augustine, into the theory that all humans shared not only Adam's sinfulness but also his guilt. Luther argued forcefully for the bondage of the human will, and the Reformed Confessions generally upheld a doctrine of total depravity, meaning that all aspects of human life were flawed rather than that there was nothing good in unredeemed human thought or action. Schleiermacher understood our predicament in terms of our loss of God-consciousness. For Karl Barth the human assumption of a false lordship made men and women 'irreparably, radically and totally guilty before Him both individually and corporately'.[40]

Clearly the many perspectives indicated in these diverse contexts are not wholly unconnected. It would appear that the various descriptions of our plight can be categorized as aspects of one or more of four basic accounts: we are an integral part of a world in which disease, corruption and death hold sway; morally and spiritually we are children who require further light, knowledge and guidance to fulfil our true destiny; we are subject to the power of evil or the demonic, manifest either through its influence on us as temptation and sinful inclination, or through the oppressive and unjust action of individuals, communities and institutions, or most insidiously through prevailing world-views with their distorting and enslaving ways of thought; or we are estranged from God.

---

[40] Karl Barth, *Church Dogmatics*, ed. by G. W. Bromiley & T. F. Torrance (Edinburgh, T&T Clark, 1985), 4.1. p. 358.

On reflection even these broad accounts are not wholly independent. First, the problem of disease, death and the decay, everywhere apparent in the created order, is linked in Christian thought with the breach in relationship that has occurred between humankind and God. It is the hope of the Church that it will be resolved in the *eschaton* even as that relation is fully re-established (see Rom 8. 18–23). Second, I doubt if there is any analysis of the human condition which would deny that we all require greater insight and understanding. This is a shared understanding common to all perspectives. Third, the theme of bondage to the power of evil and that of estrangement from God are often closely interrelated in the New Testament writings. The critical question, it seems to me, is which of these two is prior or foundational? Is the primary reality in which we find ourselves that of a radical dualism between good and evil where concerns about lordship and power predominate or is it one in which the determinative issue is the nature of our relationship with the Father and so with questions about love and accountability? In short, is our ultimate problem one of being or of relationship?[41]

In his analysis of the human predicament in Rom 1. 18–3. 20, Paul unambiguously champions the latter. Men and women are responsible to God for their actions and their estrangement from Him. They are, to use his words, 'without excuse' (1. 20, 2. 1). The light of the law, manifest in Torah and conscience, brings both Jews and Gentiles to a position where 'every mouth may be silenced and the whole world held accountable to God' (3. 19). There is no further defence that can be made for human perfidy. Our dysfunctional lives are not so much the cause of our breach with God as the consequence of it. Again and again Paul emphasizes that God has given us over to our self-indulgent ways (see 1. 24, 26, 28). Our disordered world of relationships is thus an indication of the divine decision against us. We are confronted by his wrath, not merely as a present experience but as an awesome future expectation (2. 5, 6). What then, according to Paul, is the predicament in which we find ourselves? It is that God himself as judge is standing over against us all and holding us to account, having established our culpability beyond any possible doubt. In Paul's words 'the wrath of God is being revealed' against us in the present and is 'being stored up' against us for a future day or reckoning. Paul expounds a doctrine of justification as *solution* to this our fundamental plight. We need to take his assessment of our predicament seriously if we are not to trivialize his explication of the divine response to it in Christ.

---

[41] Colin Gunton gives articulate expression to the manner in which relationship has priority over being: 'Christian theology diagnoses the ill as the disruption or distortion of the relation of personal beings with the personal creator God, a disruption that in mysterious fashion incorporates the whole created world in its structures.' *The Christian Faith: An Introduction to Christian Doctrine* (Oxford, Blackwell Publishers, 2002), p. 59.

The syntax of redemptive ideas

If lying under the judgement, condemnation or wrath of God constitutes
the essence of the human plight according to Paul, what is the nature of
the divine solution? We might well expect central place to be given to a
doctrine of forgiveness? Remarkably, however, the concept of forgiveness
is almost totally absent in the letter, only appearing in a proof-text from
Psalms as an example of the justifying act of God (Rom 4. 7). Why, in the
face of the predicament before us, does Paul not argue simply that God
forgives us, putting aside our guilt as a free and sovereign decision flowing
out of his immeasurable love for us? It is an important question which
forces us to examine his argument in the central paragraph on justification
more closely.

> God presented him as a sacrifice of atonement, through faith in
> his blood. He did this to demonstrate his justice, because in his
> forbearance he had left the sins committed beforehand unpunished
> – he did it to demonstrate his justice at the present time, so as to be
> just and the one who justifies the man who has faith in Jesus (Rom 3.
> 25, 26).

Paul finds himself confronted with a question of theodicy. How is a just God
able to leave our sins forever unpunished? Our immersion in the world-view
of the Gospel must not blind us to the ethical impropriety of the absolution
of the guilty by those in authority: 'Acquitting the guilty and condemning
the innocent – the Lord detests them both' (Prov 17. 15). Paul believes
that the doctrine of atonement that he has put forward takes seriously the
question of divine justice: how can a just God justify the ungodly? A simple
affirmation of forgiveness was clearly inadequate. Something far richer is
needed to be said.

Our intention here is not to examine how successful Paul's soteriology
was in upholding the goodness of God, but to discern how its various
components were brought together as an integrated solution to the human
predicament which he had outlined. What were those components and how
did they function together?

Justification

Paul held that all who believe in Christ are justified freely by the grace of
God. What did he mean by justification? This is probably the most carefully
examined and fiercely debated question in the history of Christian doctrine.
For the purpose of our argument it is fortunately only necessary to offer
a brief sketch of one or two aspects of Paul's thought suggested from his
own use of the expression, recognizing that the perspective put forward is
informed by my own reading of the tradition.

Paul's comparison of the effect of Christ's act of obedience with that of Adam's disobedience indicates that for him justification operates in a manner somewhat similar to that of condemnation. As one is a divine declaration of guilt, so the other is a divine declaration of innocence. But, and this is a key idea, the basis of such a declaration of innocence in his thought lies in the deeds of a third party.

> Consequently, just as the result of one trespass was condemnation for all men, so also the result of one act of righteousness was justification that brings life for all men. For just as through the disobedience of the one man the many were made sinners, so also through the obedience of the one man the many will be made righteous (Rom 5. 18, 19).

Of course this 'third party' is not some random individual. In Paul's view the whole of humankind is closely bound to Adam, even as every member of the Church is closely related or incorporated in Christ. 'For as in Adam all die, so in Christ will all be made alive' (1 Cor 15. 22). These two individuals appear to function as what some earlier theologians called 'federal heads' of their communities. As by birth we are bound into one common, fallen, Adamic humanity, so by new-birth we are by the Spirit incorporated into the renewed community of Christ. Jesus' obedience forms the basis of the divine declaration of innocence, or to use Paul's expression 'righteousness', for the believer. This new 'righteousness' is what Luther was to call an 'alien' righteousness, one that does not depend on the individual's personal obedience to the divine law, but on the obedience of Christ manifest in his willingness to suffer death. Paul's testimony to his own personal spiritual ambition emphasizes this central idea of attaining a righteousness that comes from outside of ourselves. It is one that we participate in or share in only through our participation in Christ.

> I consider them [his Jewish heritage and religious devotion] rubbish that I may gain Christ and be found in him, not having a righteousness of my own that comes from the law, but that which is through faith in Christ – the righteousness that comes from God and is by faith. (Phil 3. 8b, 9).

This matter of righteousness is, however, not just a personal issue. Paul believes that the principal reason the Jewish people as a whole have failed to attain salvation is because they have not pursued this righteousness, one which lies outside of themselves.

> ...my heart's desire and prayer for the Israelites is that they may be saved. For I can testify about them that they are zealous for God, but their zeal is not based on knowledge. Since they did not know the righteousness that comes from God, and sought to establish their own, they did not submit to God's righteousness (Rom 10. 1, 2).

This 'alien' righteousness is always seen by Paul as being intimately related to the life and death of Jesus Christ. 'God made him who had no sin to

be sin for us, so that in him we might become the righteousness of God'
(2 Cor 5. 21).

It is consequently a righteousness that not only counts with God because
it is his declaration of innocence but one that comes from God rather than
from ourselves. Some have criticized this understanding of justification
as being no more than a legal fiction, for it indicates that a person who is
quite unrighteous in the eyes of the community, considering the way he
or she has lived, is now by a divine forensic act, through faith in Christ,
considered or declared to be righteous before God. But this concern would
surely apply to any act of forgiveness. For does not forgiveness mean that
by divine absolution someone who has sinned is considered by God not to
have sinned – they are treated as innocent even though, and partly because,
they fully recognize their guilt? Scandalous as it may appear this is surely
nothing more than the message of mercy lying at the heart of the Gospel.

I would argue that in Paul's view justification functions in a manner similar
to a doctrine of forgiveness in that the problem of guilt and condemnation is
directly dealt with. It differs from it, however, in that rather than simply absolving
guilt, it affirms positively that the person in Christ has through faith a new and
alien righteousness from God, founded on the life and death of Jesus.

Redemption

What then is the relation of Jesus' life and death to the believer's new status
of innocence or righteousness? How are we to conceive of the former as
being the material cause of the latter? Paul makes use of the concept of
redemption. In the Greek world it was an everyday occurrence for payment
to be made for the redemption or manumission of a slave. The idea of
ransom or redemption was also deeply embedded in the Jewish cult and
religious tradition. The Torah indicated that a tax of half a shekel was
to be paid to the Lord by every person 'as a ransom for his life' (Exod
30. 12). The Jews believed that the firstborn belongs to the Lord but a
ransom or substitute could be offered in place of the forfeited life. Leon
Morris in his book *The Apostolic Preaching of the Cross* explains: 'Arising out
of Yahweh's claim to the firstborn is the taking of the Levites in the stead
of the firstborn (Num 3. 40ff). As there were more firstborn Israelites than
Levites, the excess, numbering 273, were redeemed by a payment of five
shekels apiece.'[42] There are other related uses of the idea of redemption
in Hebrew civil society. An ox that has gored a man should be stoned and
the owner put to death, but it is permissible for him to be redeemed by the
payment of a sum of money (Exod 21. 28ff). Equally there are occasions
when a ransom is not acceptable.

[42] Leon Morris, *The Apostolic Preaching of the Cross*, 2nd edn (London, Tyndale Press,
1960), p. 17.

> Do not accept a ransom for the life of a murderer, who deserves to die. He must surely be put to death. Do not accept a ransom for anyone who has fled to a city of refuge and so allow him to go back and live on his own land before the death of the high priest (Num 35. 31, 32).

Using this concept of ransom, Paul argues in Romans that believers 'are all justified freely by his grace through the redemption that came by Christ Jesus'. The idea is that they are set free or released from an obligation or predicament in which they find themselves through the payment of a price or substituted life. The awful and universal nature of the predicament of humankind has been carefully laid out by Paul in the previous discussion. Now through an act of redemption, or payment of a ransom, he indicates that those who have been found guilty are released from the impending judgement against them. The parallel passage in Galatians suggests that it is through the death of Christ that they find themselves delivered by him from their plight.

> Christ redeemed us from the curse of the law by becoming a curse for us, for it is written: 'Cursed be everyone who is hung on a tree' (Gal 3. 13).

The concept of redemption is thus a way of explaining how those deservedly lying under divine judgement, or its equivalent, 'the curse of the law', are liberated or released from their predicament. Redemption does not function here as an alternate theory of atonement to that of justification, but is an integral element of one rich account of the divine saving response to our universal plight.

Propitiation

The human predicament described by Paul is not simply one of human guilt or sin but has to do in the final analysis with our estrangement from God. His righteous judgement has gone out against us, his wrath has been revealed, and we are all subject to his indignation. To a faithless Israel Jeremiah declares God's promise that such anger will not last indefinitely.

> 'Return faithless Israel,' declares the Lord
> 'I will frown on you no longer, for I am merciful,' declares the Lord,
> 'I will not be angry for ever ... ' (Jer 3. 12b).

Paul employs the concept of propitiatory sacrifice as solution to this problem of divine indignation. The Jewish sacrificial system was recognized as having been given and instituted by God, but paradoxically it was in practice also a human action that had God as its object. The repentant and humbled people brought their bulls, rams and goats into God's presence on the Day of Atonement so that he might be merciful and forgive their sins. As with the intercessory prayer of the priest, the blood of the sacrificed animal is propitiatory in that it looks to God to put away his anger and show mercy to the people. It is within this framework of thought that Paul interprets the death of Christ.

> God presented him as a sacrifice of atonement (or as the one who would turn aside his wrath, taking away sin), through faith in his blood (Rom 3. 25a).

Precisely why the blood of Christ should be propitiatory, Paul does not go on to explain. But rather than looking for a new solution that stands independently of what has been said before, we should, I believe, simply refer back to his earlier argument. Jesus freely handed over his own life as ransom for the forfeited lives of the believing community and on this basis and through their close kinship with him, God is able with justice to acquit them and to grant to them a new status of righteousness in his sight based on the obedience of Christ. This act of justification thereby establishes reconciliation or peace with God (Rom 5. 1). In short, Christ's redemptive death lays the foundation for the divine justification of sinners and this in turn brings an end to the time of divine enmity. It is in this sense that the blood of Christ is propitiatory.

We have here not three theories of atonement but one. It is a mediatorial theory in which the concepts of justification, redemption and propitiation are mutually dependent and where the use of a legal metaphor is complementary to those derived from Jewish cultic sacrifice and the civil and religious practice of ransom payment. These various redemptive ideas and ways of thought are woven together by Paul to form a doctrine of atonement that finds its meaning in the whole rather than in its constituent parts. In short, the rich and integrated meaning of soteriology is disclosed in the syntax of redemptive ideas rather than in the analysis of its constituent words.

Conclusion

Justification was the central theological idea behind the Lutheran Reformation. As the *Joint Declaration* indicates it was considered by Lutherans to be the 'first and chief article' and the 'ruler and judge over all other Christian doctrines'. In the course of the sixteenth century it was also held by a number of other confessions to be the key interpretative scheme within which other soteriological perspectives could be understood. In time the doctrine of justification became an all-embracing soteriological expression and was widely considered as an equivalent to what we might now refer to simply as the doctrine of atonement. In English-speaking theology the terms redemption, reconciliation, salvation have also at times had this wide reference serving as universal soteriological concepts.

In more recent days the confidence that there might be such an overarching theory of atonement has been seriously eroded in some schools of theological thought. Synthesis has given way to analysis and comprehensive soteriological accounts have yielded to a range of comparatively independent redemptive ideas whose truth-value is relative and determined largely by their persuasive power in the various contexts in which they are used. These concepts are held to function somewhat like illustrations in a sermon in that they point to a reality other than themselves. But the content of that reality is elusive, often held to be lying beyond the realm of theological explication.

Our wider project is to encourage the search for coherence in soteriology around the concept of mediation. Here I have done no more than to indicate how Paul brought together three quite different redemptive ideas into one integrated response to the human predicament as he saw it. It shows that he had a more coherent understanding of the atonement than the variety of concepts he used might at first suggest. It also indicates how a fully developed doctrine of justification is able to go far beyond the use of legal terminology and concepts and is able to provide an interpretative scheme within which other redemptive themes play a part. In short it provides the framework for a unified theory of the atonement in which Christ's saving ministry is recognized as mediating our peace with God.

5

The Place of Faith in Reconciliation

I have argued that the various soteriological themes in the New Testament including the defeat of radical evil, the end of death's tyranny, the revelation of divine love in the gift of God's Son to the world, the forgiveness of sins, the justification of the ungodly, the redemption of those whose lives have been forfeited and the propitiation of the Father are not so many independent or unconnected accounts of salvation. Rather, the concept of Christ as mediator is able to disclose their coherent relationship within the framework of what may be described as a mediatorial theory of the atonement. This interpretative theory has been summarized in a master-story which, allowing for certain perspectives arising from the discussion of the last two chapters, now takes the following form:

> *The Father gave his only Son to become as we are so that, in offering up himself on our behalf through the Spirit, he might reconcile us to God.*

Attention has already been drawn to the way in which the Church Fathers used the phrase 'the Word became flesh' or the concept of 'incarnation' as their main hermeneutic principle in christology. It did not curtail the debate but gave it focus, bringing clarity to the central issues. Of course the time may come when a particular master-story is no longer considered as the most helpful interpretative theory in its field of knowledge and is either reformulated or changed radically. The 'search for the historical Jesus' in the eighteenth and nineteenth centuries was in part driven by the concern of a number of scholars that an incarnational model of Christ failed to give adequate account of Jesus' Spirit-empowered human life among us. It was tacitly replaced by them with an 'inspirational' master-story of the form: Jesus of Nazareth was a man sent by God among you, filled with the Holy Spirit. Karl Barth later offered a rather different christological key when he explicated the person of Christ in terms of the Word of God or God's self-revelation. It provided his school with a quite new hermeneutic principle by which related theological themes could be explicated. This shift from one interpretative model to another has been more frequent in the historical development of soteriology which only began to be formulated with some precision through the controversies of the twelfth century.[43] Principal

---

[43] J. N. D. Kelly makes the point well: 'The student who seeks to understand the soteriology of the fourth and fifth centuries will be sharply disappointed if he expects to find anything corresponding to the elaborately worked out syntheses which the contemporary theology of the Trinity and the Incarnation presents. In both these latter departments controversy forced fairly exact definition on the Church, whereas the redemption did not

among the models used by the Church in this field have been the concepts of recapitulation, divinization, redemption, satisfaction, justification and in more recent times, revelation. Perhaps the present lack of soteriological clarity in academic theology is simply that there is now no single, generally recognized, redemptive master-story or model.

The argument of this book has been that the concept of Christ as mediator is the appropriate interpretative key to soteriology. It is an argument which is not primarily dependent on the question of whether this age finds these ideas easy to understand or assimilate into its current world-view. It is rather that such a theory discloses most clearly the inner rationality of soteriological thought in the New Testament and incorporates many of the deepest insights of Christian reflection over the centuries. There is certainly no attempt at novelty in our argument that the Son became as we are so as to make peace with the Father.

But how can we test this? Other than in its ability to offer a coherent account of the material before it, how can one assess the value of a theory of atonement? I have suggested earlier that one mark of an effective theory is that it is fruitful or illuminating in wider application. Let us examine then how well a mediatorial view of the atonement integrates with related theological themes.

There is clearly a close relation between the Father's gracious intention for his people; the life, death and resurrection of Jesus of Nazareth; the proclamation of these events by the Church; the enlightening and trans-forming work of the Holy Spirit; the respondent faith in the hearts of those who hear the message; their new relation of peace or favour with God; and all the spiritual benefits that flow from it. The field of theological thought, in which the interdependence of these themes is considered is sometimes described as the *ordo salutis* or 'way of salvation'. Let us begin by considering the relation of the atonement, understood as mediatory, to the response required of those who hear it proclaimed. But first we must ask, 'What is that required response?'

Faith and reconciliation

In the Book of Acts, Luke gives an account of the dramatic conversion of a Philippian gaoler. Terrified by an earthquake the gaoler comes before two of his prisoners, Paul and Silas, and asks: 'Sirs, what must I do to be saved?' They reply, 'Believe in the Lord Jesus, and you will be saved – you and your household' (Acts 16. 30b, 31). The straightforward connection suggested here between belief and salvation is affirmed throughout much of the New Testament. It is particularly clear in the Johannine corpus: 'Yet

---

become a battle-ground for the rival schools until the twelfth century, when Anselm's *Cur deus homo* (c. 1097) focussed attention on it.' *Early Christian Doctrines,* 5th edn (London, Adam & Charles Black, 1977), p. 375.

to all who received him, to those who believed in his name, he gave the right to become the children of God ...' (John 1. 12) and 'Whoever believes in him is not condemned, but whoever does not believe stands condemned already, because they have not believed in the name of God's one and only Son' (John 3. 18). Paul uses the word 'trust' and more often 'faith' along with that of 'belief' in delineating the human response to the gospel: '...to anyone who does not work but trusts God who justifies the ungodly, their faith is credited as righteousness' (Rom 4. 5) and 'Does God give you his Spirit and work miracles among you by your observing the law, or by your believing what you heard?' (Gal 3. 5). The writer to the Hebrews warns his readers of the consequence of not exercising such faith: 'Therefore, since the promise of entering his rest still stands, let us be careful that none of you be found to have fallen short of it. For we also have had the gospel preached to us, just as they did; but the message they heard was of no value to them, because those who heard did not combine it with faith. Now we who have believed enter that rest ... ' (Heb 4. 1–3a).

That the experience of salvation is closely related in New Testament thought to the exercise of faith is clear. What is not so apparent is the actual role played by such faith in effecting salvation. The following questions highlight the problem. If Christ has indeed effected peace with God, what need is there for the gospel to be preached? If reconciliation has already been achieved through the cross, why are human repentance and faith considered necessary for its appropriation?

Pelagianism and the medieval discussion

One answer might be that faith is required of us because our reconciliation with God is achieved in part through what Christ has done and in part through our own believing response to his work. Over the centuries many Christians have had great difficulty with this apparently straightforward solution for they have seen in it an implication that humans are able, at least in part, to achieve or earn salvation by their own act of faith.

This concern was highlighted in the controversy between Augustine and Pelagius in the early fifth century. The whole matter turned on the question of whether the unaided human will was able to effect any spiritual good and the extent to which it had been debilitated by the Fall. The British monk Pelagius, disturbed by the growing moral laxity of the Church, argued for the freedom of human volition and so for our ability to resist sin.

> We distinguish [says he] three things, arranging them in a certain graduated order. We put in the first place 'ability;' in the second, 'volition;' and in the third, 'actuality.' The 'ability' we place in our nature, the 'volition' in our will, and the 'actuality' in the effect. The first, that is, the 'ability,' properly belongs to God, who has bestowed it on His creature; the other two, that is, the 'volition' and the 'actuality,'

must be referred to man, because they flow forth from the fountain of the will... [W]henever we say that a man can live without sin, we also give praise to God by our acknowledgment of the capacity which we have received from Him, who has bestowed such 'ability' upon us ...[44]

Augustine was also concerned with the moral health of the Church but his view of human nature was far more pessimistic. He believed that through Adam's sin the whole human race had become sinful and such sin was passed on from parent to child. In particular the liberty to avoid sin and to will and do that which was good had now been lost. It is not so much that human volition is not free intrinsically, it is rather that since the Fall, it lies under necessity to do only what is wrong. 'It came by the freedom of choice that man was with sin; but a penal corruption closely followed thereon, and out of the liberty produced necessity.'[45] For Augustine this necessity is thus a psychological rather than a metaphysical determinism, a bondage of the will that can be overcome only by grace.[46]

The Church gave general support to Augustine's position in this matter, anathematised Pelagius' teaching at the Council of Carthage in 418 and condemned his disciple Caelestius at the Council of Ephesus in 431. There were those like John Cassian who sought a mediating position, arguing that the initial movement of faith is the sinner's own, yet it is a movement that grace goes on to assist. However, in due course even they were considered as semi-Pelagian and their position discredited.[47]

Preparation of the soul

This widespread belief that fallen humans have no ability in themselves to respond appropriately to God, meant that faith came to be viewed as a divine gift, a new ability quite independent of human volition. 'Believing' was therefore not something a person could simply choose to do, it was rather an 'habitual grace' given by God. But with such an understanding of faith, what place was left for a human response to the gospel? Augustine's celebrated dictum: 'He who made you without your cooperation will not

---

[44] Augustine, *A Treatise on the Grace of Christ and on Original Sin*, from A Select Library of the Nicene and Post-Nicene Fathers of the Christian Church, ed. by Philip Schaff, vol. 5 (Grand Rapids, Wm B. Eerdmans), I, 5.

[45] Augustine, *A Treatise Concerning Man's Perfection in Righteousness*, NP–NF, vol. 5, p. 9.

[46] Alister McGrath helpfully outlines Augustine's position: 'Although Adam possessed *liberum arbitrium* before the Fall, man's free will is now compromised by sin, so that it is now *liberum arbitrium captivatum*. The free will is not lost, nor is it non-existent: it is merely incapacitated, and may be healed by grace. In justification, the *liberum arbitrium captivatum* becomes the *liberum arbitrium liberatum* by the action of healing grace. *Iustitia Dei: A History of the Christian Doctrine of Justification,* 2nd edn (Cambridge, Cambridge University Press, 2000), pp. 26, 27.

[47] See J. N. D. Kelly, *Early Christian Doctrines*, 5th edn (London, Adam & Charles Black, 1977), pp. 370, 371.

save you without it'[48] (Sermons 169, 13), ensured that this question was not simply discarded by the medieval Church. How did it then explain the nature of the subjective human response to the gospel? It could not do so in terms of faith, for this was seen as God's gift, a divine grace lying outside of human willing. Rather the Church considered the preparation of the soul to receive such grace as the theatre of human participation in the process of salvation. And it was the theological implications of this idea which engaged the mind of the 'schools' through much of the Middle Ages.

The difficulty that faced them was to show how one could speak of a human preparation for grace without falling into the trap of Pelagianism outlined above, that is, the idea that humans had the ability in themselves to contribute to their salvation. The medieval Church showed great ingenuity in illustrating how this might be done within a broadly Augustinian theological framework as McGrath indicates.

> Peter of Poitiers used a domestic analogy to illustrate the role of such a preparation for justification. A man may clean out his house and decorate it in order to receive an important guest, so that all will be ready when he arrives. This preparation however, does not necessitate the arrival of the guest, which depends only upon the guest's love for his host ... According to Alan (of Lille), man's preparation for justification could be likened to opening a shutter to let sunlight into a room. The act of penitence was the *causa sine qua non* and the occasion, but not the *causa efficiens*, of justification.[49]

The problem was that the Church's theologians were also astute enough to recognize that whatever role was ascribed to unaided human endeavour in the process of salvation, it was bound to entail some form of Pelagianism, for it inevitably implied that the human will had the capability to do something on its own to effect salvation. Thomas Aquinas in his mature writing argued that whatever preparation was made for the soul to receive grace, it could itself only come about through the gracious agency of God. But he strongly denied that this would imply an infinite regression of God's grace – the giving of grace to prepare the soul to receive grace.

> Now in order that man prepare himself to receive this gift, it is not necessary to presuppose any further habitual gift in the soul, otherwise we should go on to infinity. But we must presuppose a gratuitous gift of God, Who moves the soul inwardly or inspires the good wish (*Summa Theologica*, II. 1. q. 109. 6).

Now if the preparation required for the soul to receive faith or divine grace is itself held to flow out of an act of God's grace, one wonders whether Aquinas is justified in his denial of the need for an infinite regression of

---

[48] Qui fecit te sine te, non te justificat sine te.
[49] Alister E. McGrath, *Iustitia Dei: A History of the Christian Doctrine of Justification,* 2nd edn (Cambridge, Cambridge University Press, 2000), pp. 78, 84.

the giving of grace. However charitably one views his position here, it is clear that the broader argument has lost its way. The introduction of the idea of the preparation of the soul to receive the grace of faith was done precisely to explain what part humans played in the saving process. But if this preparation is itself now recognized as an act of grace, this whole theological detour has taken us back to where we started, that is, looking for the human or subjective element in salvation. A completely different approach to the question of faith's relation to salvation was required and it is instructive to see how Martin Luther was able to do this.

Luther

Luther's estimate of the freedom of the human will, expounded forcefully in *The Bondage of the Will* as a response to Erasmus' *Diatribe on Free-will* was even more pessimistic and deterministic than that of Augustine. He argued that free will applies ultimately only to the Divine Majesty.[50] Apart from God's grace humans have no ability to choose the good. Their bondage lies not merely in their sinfulness but in their creatureliness. They simply do not have the power in themselves to respond positively to God. But this lack of free will, rather than being problematic for his understanding of faith, served to inspire his Christian hope.

> I frankly confess that, for myself, even if it could be, I should not want 'free-will' to be given me, nor anything to be left in my own hands to endeavour after salvation … If I lived and worked to all eternity, my conscience would never reach comfortable certainty as to how much it must do to satisfy God … But now that God has taken my salvation out of the control of my own will, and put it under the control of His, and promised to save me, not according to my working or running, but according to His own grace and mercy, I have the comfortable certainty that He is faithful … (*The Bondage of the Will*, Dillenberger, p. 199).

Luther argues strongly for a doctrine of divine sovereignty and human powerlessness precisely so that he and his hearers might be encouraged to look away from themselves and towards God alone for salvation. He does in effect turn the whole discussion on its head. Creaturely inability to achieve anything of spiritual value instead of being problematic for his understanding of faith is actually an impetus to the exercise of justifying faith. He has moved from an Augustinian and somewhat intellectualist understanding of faith as an apprehension of the Christian body of truth to a more existentialist interpretation of faith as a looking away from self and taking hold of Christ for salvation.

[50] See Martin Luther, *Selections from his Writings*, ed. by John Dillenberger (New York, Anchor Books, 1961), p. 188.

> The third incomparable benefit of faith is that it unites the soul with Christ as a bride is united with her bridegroom ... Christ is full of grace, life and salvation. The soul is full of sins, death and damnation. Now let faith come between them and sins, death and damnation will be Christ's, while grace, life and salvation will be the souls', for if Christ is a bridegroom, he must take upon himself the things which are his bride's and bestow upon her the things that are his (*Freedom of a Christian*, Dillenberger, p. 60).

We catch a glimpse here of how faith functions soteriologically in Luther's thought. Faith is that which links believers to Christ; that which enables them to share in his richness, while he takes upon himself their poverty. It is closely related to his principal model of atonement which is the justification of the sinner through the alien righteousness of Christ. By faith the righteousness of Christ becomes the new righteousness of the believer. The hearer of the gospel is urged to take hold of Christ and all his benefits. Through faith Christ is made present to them. The inability of the sinner to do anything worthy of God, far from being a reason for despondency is a spur for them to place their hope not in themselves but in Jesus.

Luther asserts that humans are unable to do anything of spiritual value and that faith is a divine gift. Yet, in his soteriology, these convictions do not undermine the call on the hearer of the gospel to believe or take hold of Christ, rather they provide a stimulus for such action. He thereby opened a path which leads us out of the circular and somewhat sterile scholastic debate about preparation for grace and takes an important step towards the world of ideas that informed the New Testament writers and preachers.

The nature of faith

Let us summarise some of the principles arising from this discussion relating to the parameters of faith.

1. *Faith is a gift of God.* It is a human faculty that lies outside of fallen human possibilities.
2. *Faith is the appropriate human response to the gospel.* The subjective or human element in the process of salvation is to be located here rather than in some prior preparation of the soul to receive grace.
3. *Faith looks away from itself and towards God alone for salvation.* A faith that focuses on its own efficacy or significance is a perversion of itself. Consequently faith must not be viewed as the cause or ground of our salvation. This is rather to be found in the work of Christ, flowing out of God's love for us.

These three principles can be considered as part of the skeleton or underlying structure of an adequate doctrine of faith. Held together they form a framework that gives shape to a doctrine that is always in danger of falling over in one theological direction at the cost of another. When one of them is weakened the whole structure tends to topple. Viewed from this perspective Pelagianism can be seen as a failure to affirm the first principle. Scholasticism, broadly speaking, did not take due account of the second. Fideism, the focus on faith as the cause of our salvation and the subtle temptation into which a doctrine of justification by faith can sometimes be in danger of falling, arises from a neglect of the third.

Considered individually, these principles appear as natural and non-contentious presentations of the biblical testimony to the working of faith. The difficulty lies in holding them together. Their seemingly paradoxical nature when considered together has meant that one or other of these principles has tended to be discarded in either the theology or the practice of the Christian community, as the following examples indicate.

Arminianism

Famous for its challenge to the strict Calvinism practised in Holland in the sixteenth century, Arminianism is often viewed as a form of Pelagianism. It is therefore somewhat surprising to discover just how clear both Arminius and the Arminian Remonstrant Articles are in denying freedom to the fallen human will to achieve anything of spiritual value.

> But in his lapsed and sinful state, man is not capable, of and by himself, either to think, to will, or to do that which is really good; but it is necessary for him to be regenerated and renewed in his intellect, affections or will, and in all his powers, by God in Christ through the Holy Spirit, that he may be qualified rightly to understand, esteem, consider, will, and perform whatever is truly good[51] (Arminius).
>
> That this grace of God is the beginning, continuance, and accomplishment of all good, even to this extent, that the regenerate man himself, without prevenient or assisting, awakening, following and cooperative grace, can neither think, will, nor do good, nor withstand any temptations to evil; so that all good deeds or movements, that can be conceived, must be ascribed to the grace of God in Christ. But respecting the mode of the operation of this grace, it is not irresistible; inasmuch as it is written concerning many, that they have resisted the Holy Ghost (Acts 7) and elsewhere in many places (Remonstrant Articles, 4).

The point of issue that the Arminians had with contemporary Calvinism in this particular matter was that God's saving grace was held to be resistible. A minor and non-controversial point one might feel in the greater scheme

---

[51] Arminius, *A declaration of the sentiments of Arminius on: III. Freedom of the Will.* Works of J. Arminius, vol. 1.

of theological thought. But we need to consider for a moment what their position implies for the process of salvation. The sinner, it is argued, has the freedom to reject, or by implication to choose to receive the grace of God, a grace that leads to faith and so to salvation. But the stage in which this vital choice is made lies outside the reaches of grace. Salvation ultimately depends on this spiritually unaided human decision – the decision whether to resist or to accept grace. The link with Pelagianism is apparent. At the critical moment the hearers of the gospel stand on their own, separate from the gracious work of the Holy Spirit. The momentous act which they make towards salvation is an unaided human choice. Faith is conceded as God's gift, but the significant subjective response is held to lie not in the act of faith but in the prior decision to reject or accept divine grace.

This 'Arminian' pattern is apparent in the contemporary Church wherever the response to the proclamation of the gospel is considered primarily as an act of human volition, a decision of commitment to Christ, of obedience to the divine call, a personal choice to be baptized or join the Church, particularly when these acts of the will are held to lie within the range of fallen human possibilities. There is in this theological framework a failure to recognize, as in (2), that the theatre of human response has to do, not so much with a decision of the will, as with the exercise of faith in God's grace, and that this faith is itself a work of the Holy Spirit, a gift of God (1). The dynamic and content of such faith will be considered in due course.

The Faith of Christ

The most radical challenge in recent times to the structure of faith outlined above has come from a quite different quarter. Some forty or so years ago Thomas Torrance articulated the concept of the faith or faithfulness of Christ as the appropriate human response to God: 'He believed for us, offering to God in His vicarious faithfulness, the perfect response of human faith which we could not offer.'[52]

The seed of this idea is to be found in Rom 5. 18, 19 where Paul argues that through Christ's one act of obedience many will be justified. The idea was developed in Irenaeus' theory of recapitulation in which Christ as the second Adam is held to have encapsulated in himself the whole of humanity and passing through the various stages of human life sanctified each of them in turn, accomplishing for us what either we or Adam had failed to do. In the seventeenth century Johannes Cocceius helped to formalize, through his 'Federal theology', the theory that Christ fulfilled on our behalf a covenant of works, as our federal head, offering to God the obedience that Adam had failed to bring. This view, which played a major

[52] Thomas F. Torrance, *God and Rationality* (London, Oxford University Press, 1971), p. 154.

influence in later Reformed theology, maintained that both Christ's active obedience (faithful life) and passive obedience (death on the cross) were required for our reconciliation with God.

However, the view that Christ not only offered to God a life of obedience or faithfulness as our representative, but actually believed in our place, had its particular roots, as far as I am aware, in the theology of John McLeod Campbell writing in the latter part of the nineteenth century. Campbell sought a way of explaining Jesus' atoning action within a mediatorial framework, but was anxious to avoid any suggestion of Jesus directly suffering divine judgement or punishment. He did so by proposing that atonement was accomplished through Christ's confession of our sins in our stead.

> ... meeting the cry of these sins for judgment, and the wrath due to them, absorbing and exhausting that divine wrath in that adequate confession and perfect response on the part of man, which was possible only to the infinite and eternal righteousness in humanity.[53]

Torrance, following a similar direction to that taken by Karl Barth,[54] eloquently developed this idea of Christ confessing our sins in our stead, into one of Christ believing on our behalf.

> Thus Jesus steps into the actual situation where we are summoned to have faith in God, to believe and trust in him, and he acts in our place and in our stead from within the depths of our unfaithfulness and provides us freely with a faithfulness in which we may share ... That is to say, if we think of belief, trust or faith as forms of human activity before God, then we must think of Jesus Christ as believing, trusting and having faith in God the Father on our behalf and in our place (*The Mediation of Christ*, pp. 82, 83).

How are we to respond to this rather original[55] and somewhat strange-sounding idea that Jesus believes in our place? It appears odd as soon as we try to ground the idea in the reality of the religious life of Jesus. The content of Christian faith is summarized in this early formula of the Church:

> By this gospel you are saved, if you hold firmly to the word I preached to you. Otherwise, you have believed in vain. For what I received I passed on to you as of first importance: that Christ died for our sins

---

[53] John McLeod Campbell, *The Nature of the Atonement and its relation to the Remission of Sins and Eternal Life* (London, Macmillan & Co., 1878), p. 125.

[54] Karl Barth argued that our faith was to be understood in terms of Jesus Christ's life. 'We shall speak correctly of the faith and love and hope of the individual Christian only when it remains clear and constantly becomes clear that, although we are dealing with our existence, we are dealing with our existence in Jesus Christ as our true existence, that we are therefore dealing with Him and not with us, and with us only in so far as absolutely and exclusively with Him.' CD IV.1 p.154.

[55] Some German biblical scholars including G. Kittel had advocated a subjective genitive interpretation of *pistis christou* earlier in the twentieth century.

according to the Scriptures, that he was buried, that he was raised on the third day ... (1 Cor 15. 2–4a).

Now if Jesus actually did in his life among us what we are called to do, what was the content of his faith? Was it in any way like ours? He clearly could not trust that Christ died for his sins. The difficulty is compounded if we consider the existential element of faith in terms such as a taking hold of Christ and his benefits as suggested by Luther's metaphor of marriage. It stretches our conceptual skills to make sense of the notion that Christ in his humanity 'grasped' or 'received' Christ and his benefits on our behalf?

However absurd it may appear, this idea that Christ believed on our behalf has not been put forward lightly or without regard to the 'rule of faith'. Torrance is a careful, serious and acclaimed Reformed theologian, deeply committed to upholding the apostolic faith of the Church. Why then does he take this paradoxical step of arguing that Christ believes in our stead?

First, Torrance's soteriology is firmly based on the idea of Christ as mediator. He rightly emphasizes the role of the Son's vicarious humanity as the agent of our reconciliation with God and fully appreciates the emphasis in the letter to the Hebrews that Christ as man enters the presence of God on our behalf. The underlying logic of his theology is that through his humanity Christ does what we could not do, establishing peace with the Father. Christ stands for us before God. Few modern scholars have so clearly grasped the soteriological significance of this New Testament theme.

Second, Torrance is rightly concerned with the dangers of 'synergism', the idea that we contribute in part to our salvation, and of 'fideism', the tendency to focus on our own faith as the significant element in the redemptive process. In short, he is supportive of the direction of the first and third principles of our structure of faith outlined above. Like Luther, he is consequently unwilling to allow any grounds for the hearers of the gospel to look to themselves for their salvation. But whereas Luther emphasized the total inability of fallen humans to do anything of spiritual value, Torrance, developing the idea of the vicarious nature of Christ's ministry, argues that everything required for salvation has already been accomplished by Christ. This, he argues, includes the human response of faith. The intention of Luther and Torrance is the same: men and women must not look to themselves for salvation. Luther says they have no ability to do it; Torrance, that they have no need to do it.

But Torrance's strategy actually turns out to be far more like that of the medieval Scholastics. To avoid Pelagianism, they in effect removed faith from the theatre of human response. The vacant space which this left was filled by a new human activity – the preparation of the soul to receive grace. But we saw how all the original difficulties associated with the role of faith returned to perplex those who took this route. Torrance also removes faith from the sphere of appropriate human response, making it a ministry of Christ. But the critical question then is: what fills the empty space?

> Hence the proclamation of the Gospel announces to us that the true
> and faithful response of man to God has already been made in the
> self-offering of Christ on our behalf, and holds it out to us as the
> divinely appointed and provided response in which we may share
> freely as through the Spirit we participate in the vicarious obedience
> of the Word made flesh (*The Mediation of Christ*, pp. 152, 153).

But how are we to share in Christ's response? How are we to participate in
his faithfulness? Is it by obedience to Christ the Lord; is it by imitation of
the life of Christ; is it by faith in his atoning work? All the old questions
simply reappear at this new level. Torrance indicates that we participate in
Christ's faithfulness through our own act of faith. It is by our believing that
Christ believed for us.

> Hence our response of faith is made within the ring of faithfulness
> which Christ has already thrown around us, when in faith we rely not
> on our own believing but wholly on His vicarious response of faith-
> fulness toward God (p. 154).

I am not sure that Torrance is fully aware of the extent to which he
has undermined his own argument. He originally ascribed the human
response of faith to Jesus as part of a theological strategy. He was unwilling
to concede that we play any role in responding to the gospel, because in his
view our salvation would then depend in some measure on us. That is why
he argued that in his vicarious humanity Jesus had done absolutely everything for us including believing in our stead. It is clear that such a strategy
can not allow even the smallest element in the process of salvation to be
ascribed to our own subjective response. Torrance is caught in precisely the
same trap as the Scholastics were when they moved their focus away from
the human response of faith to the preparation of the soul to receive grace.
The same set of problems simply reappears at a different level. How does
one prepare the soul to receive grace apart from divine grace? How are we
able to believe that Jesus has believed for us? Is it something we are left to
do on our own? Does Jesus not step in and believe even these things in our
stead? We are faced with the absurdity of an infinite regression of Christ
believing for us. On the other hand, if it is argued, as Torrance appears to,
that we are also required in our own right to believe, then we have been
brought back to where we started, seeking to understand the working of
that faith, a faith that is not to be ascribed to Christ.[56]

---

[56] It is instructive to see how Torrance, in his presentation of the Gospel, is constrained
to call his hearers to exercise faith even as he argues that Christ has believed for them.
'God loves you so utterly and completely that he has given himself for you in Jesus Christ
his beloved Son, and has thereby pledged his very being as God for your salvation ... Jesus
Christ died for you precisely because you are sinful and unworthy of him, and has thereby
already made you his own before and apart from your ever believing in him. He has bound
you to himself by his love in a way that he will never let you go, for even if you refuse him
and damn yourself in hell his love will never cease. *Therefore, repent and believe in Jesus Christ
as your Lord and Saviour* ... He has acted in your place in the whole range of your human

Torrance's strategy, like that of the Scholastics, patently fails. There is no coherent alternative to the overwhelming testimony of the Scriptures that faith is *our* appropriate response to the gospel. This is the reality with which soteriological reflection has to deal and it is not to be neatly sidestepped by a theological sleight of hand. We need rather to consider how we might articulate the dynamic and content of such faith in a way that does not veer into either Pelagianism or fideism. Before we do so, let us briefly consider an objection to our argument above.

Pistis christou

There are a number of New Testament scholars today who would contend that phrases of the form *pistis christou*, which occur some seven times in Romans, Galatians and Philippians, should be translated as the 'faith or faithfulness of Jesus Christ', rather than 'faith in Jesus Christ' as they are in most English Bibles, and that these provide a firm biblical base for the view that Christ believed in our stead.

It would seem, however, that the process actually moves in the opposite direction. Since the publication in 1983 of his book *The Faith of Jesus Christ*, Richard Hays has been a leading proponent of the view that *pistis christou* refers to the faith or faithfulness of Christ. In a more recent published discussion with James Dunn he concedes that 'the syntactical arguments are, however, finally inconclusive' and makes the following assessment.

> Our interpretative decision about the meaning of Paul's phrase, therefore, must be governed by larger judgements about the shape and logic of Paul's thought concerning faith, Christ and salvation. Indeed, rather than defining the debate as a dispute between subjective genitive and objective genitive readings, we would do better to speak – as some recent essays have suggested – of a distinction between the christological and anthropological interpretations of *pistis christou*. The christological reading highlights the salvific efficacy of Jesus Christ's faith(fullness) for God's people; the anthropological reading stresses the salvific efficacy of the human act of faith directed towards Jesus.[57]

---

life and activity, including your personal decisions, and your responses to God's love, and even your acts of faith. He has believed for you, fulfilled your human response to God, even made your personal decision for you, so that he acknowledges you before God as one who has already responded to God in him, who has already believed in God through him, and whose personal decision is already implicated in Christ's self-offering to the Father. In all of which he has been fully and completely accepted by the Father, so that in Jesus Christ you are already accepted by him. *Therefore, renounce yourself, take up your cross and follow Jesus as Lord and Saviour.*'(italics mine.) *The Mediation of Christ*, p. 94.

[57] Richard B. Hays, 'PISTIS and Pauline Christology: What is at stake?', *Pauline Theology*, vol, 4, ed. by E. Elizabeth Johnson & David M. Hay, (Atlanta, Georgia, Scholars Press, 1997), pp. 39, 40.

This is a helpful analysis. Hays recognizes that the whole debate is being driven by a theological issue which has to do with the role of human faith in the process of salvation and a concern that an emphasis on such human faith might undermine the efficacy of Christ's redemptive work. He believes that the interpretation of *pistis christou* as the 'faith or faithfulness of Jesus' is required if we are to counter the implication that the human act of faith is in itself meritorious in salvation. In short, if Torrance's theory is correct we are constrained to look at the texts in this way and so avoid a synergistic understanding of redemption. But if Torrance is wrong, as he clearly appears to be, the entire project is undermined.[58]

The dynamic of faith

Let us consider then how the functioning of human faith can be explained in such a way that it does not undermine the efficacy of Christ's atoning work. One can begin by asking: why is human faith particularly appropriate as the human response to the gospel?

The nominalist response is that this is simply how God has arranged it. William Courtenay gives an outline of how nominalism works as a theological principle. 'Causal efficacy results not from forces or inherent virtues placed within created things but rather from a value which God ascribes to things and which he rewards on the basis of covenant or agreement with creation and the church.'[59] Theoretically it would seem that 'love' could have been the characteristic human attribute through which redemption was appropriated if God had so determined it in his covenant with humankind. The Puritan Thomas Watson illustrates the idea:

> Therefore God has put this honour on faith, to make it saving and justifying. The king's stamp makes the coin pass for current; if he would put his stamp upon leather, as well as silver, it would make it

---

[58] James Dunn holds a similar theological position to Hays, but finds that he is unable to interpret *pistis christou* in a way which would support such a perspective. Consequently, his carefully worded conclusion to the discussion of its meaning carries particular weight. 'I should make it clear that the *theology* of the subjective genitive reading is powerful, important and attractive. For anyone who wishes to take the humanness of Jesus with full seriousness "the faith of Jesus" strikes a strong resonant cord. Moreover, as a theological motif, it seems to me wholly compatible with Paul's theology but consistent with other emphases. As Hooker has noted, it follows naturally when we bring together the thought of God in Christ and the thought of God's faithfulness. It is an attractive variant on the Adam motif on Christ's obedience. None of this, however, is to the particular point at dispute. That focuses on the meaning Paul intended when he dictated the phrase *pistis christou*. And on this point I remain wholly convinced that Paul intended his audiences to hear that phrase in the sense in the sense "faith in Christ".' 'Once More PISTIS CHRISTOU' in *Pauline Theology*, vol. 4, ed. by E. Elizabeth Johnson & David M. Hay (Atlanta, Georgia, Scholars Press, 1997), p. 79.

[59] William Courtenay, 'Nominalism', in *A New Dictionary of Christian Theology*, ed. by Alan Richardson & John Bowden, (London, SCM Press Ltd, 1985), p. 404.

current: so God having put his sanction, the stamp of his authority and institution upon faith, makes it to be justifying and saving.[60]

Nominalism does not require a particular 'fit' of faith and the gospel. The efficacy of faith is ultimately by divine determination rather than by its inherent function or suitability in the process of salvation. Such a theory allows faith to be interpreted as a predominantly intellectual matter, an assent to revealed truth, without any question being raised as to why such an assent should be instrumental in salvation. Calvin's classic formulation of faith takes this outward shape:

> We shall now have a full definition of faith if we say that it is a firm and sure knowledge of the divine favour toward us, founded on the truth of a free promise in Christ, and revealed to our minds, and sealed on our hearts, by the Holy Spirit (III. 2. 7).

Faith is in essence a type of knowledge, but why knowledge should be necessary for eternal salvation is a question that is not immediately apparent, nor is it explored. It is quite different with Luther's more dynamic or existential view of faith outlined above and sometimes explained as a 'marrying' or 'taking hold' of Christ. In Luther's account the relation of the act of faith to the appropriation of redemption is clear. We remember that his doctrine of justification is largely transactional. By receiving the external righteousness of Christ the sinner is justified. Through faith all the benefits of Christ and all the privileges associated with him become those of the believer. The power of the concepts of 'marriage' or 'grasping Christ' as metaphors for faith is not just that they point away from themselves to the worthiness of the Redeemer, but they help us to conceive why faith is instrumentally efficacious – why it 'works'.

How does one decide between a nominalist understanding of the instrumental efficacy of faith as dependent on divine decree and a more existential interpretation of faith which holds that there is a dynamic and natural relation between faith, the gospel and salvation? It might be helpful to look afresh at the way Paul viewed this matter?

Faith and promise

In the ninth chapter of Romans, Paul explains why God's word to the Israelites has not failed even though so many of them had rejected the Christian gospel. His initial line of argument is that not all Israelite descendants are actually part of the true Israel, a position he is able to defend by reference to Israel's genealogy. From their own Scriptural record it is clear that not all the children born to either Abraham or Isaac were considered as heirs of the divine covenant. What is it then that marks off

[60] Thomas Watson, *A Body of Divinity*, (London, Banner of Trust, 1965), p. 218.

one child from another, why should one be considered a true Israelite and not the other? Paul makes an important distinction between natural children and children of promise, and it is upon this distinction that much of his soteriology turns.

> In other words it is not the natural children who are God's children, but it is the children of the promise who are regarded as Abraham's offspring (Rom 9. 8).

The distinction flows from Paul's understanding of the sovereignty or freedom of God in redemption. Salvation comes not from human descent or human action but from a divine decision to be merciful (vv. 10–12). It all has to do with God. Paul is quite aware that his argument raises issues of theodicy and we misunderstand him if we interpret him to suggest that it doesn't. His blunt response to those of us troubled by such questions is that as creatures it is inappropriate for us to ask them (vv. 19–21). Like Augustine and Luther he looks away from any human ability or attribute as a ground for salvation. It all depends on God's grace, on God's mercy, on God's promise.

The paradigmatic child of promise is of course Isaac. 'For it is written that Abraham had two sons, one by the slave woman and the other by the free woman. His son by the slave woman was born as the result of human effort, but his son by the free woman was born as the result of a divine promise' (Gal 4: 22, 23). This is why the great age of Isaac's parents in the narrative is emphasized. They were as good as dead. The birth of the boy was clearly an act of God, Isaac was a child of promise.

The significance of the concept of promise is not just a Pauline theological idea but is one that lies at the heart of nearly all aspects of both Jewish and Christian religious life. The covenant is understood as a divine initiative founded on God's promise. Israel is the land of promise. The temple is built by Solomon according to the promise made to David. The Davidic line is held to be secure according to divine promise. The hope of a restoration from exile is based on God's promise. In the New Testament the Holy Spirit is sometimes spoken of simply as 'the promise' (Acts 2. 39). It is through God's promises that we experience salvation: 'Through these he has given us his very great and precious promises, so that through them you may participate in the divine nature, having escaped the corruption that is in the world' (2 Pet 1. 4).

Now the particular power of Paul's soteriology lies in the close connection he made between justifying faith and the idea of promise. As Isaac is the exemplar of promise, so Abraham provides the pattern of faith, he is the father of all who believe. The two concepts become intertwined. The promise of Isaac is fulfilled through the faith of Abraham. The faith of Abraham is trust in the promise of Isaac. If we are to understand the nature or working of faith we need to consider Abraham's response to the divine promise – a promise that indirectly points towards Christ (see Gal 3. 16). From him we learn that justifying faith is more than intellectual assent, it is wholehearted trust in the divine promise, the promise of an inheritance, ultimately the promise of salvation. It is a deep assurance that what God has promised he will bring about (Rom 4. 21). It is a belief in the fulfilment of this promise against impossible odds (v. 18). It is the conviction that life can be generated from that which is already dead (v. 17), it is what we might call a type of resurrection hope. It is a trust that inevitably results in a new way of life, a life of loyalty and obedience.

Paul, then, understands faith primarily as trust in the divine promise. It is for him more than new and certain knowledge. By it God's gracious promise is accepted, held on to, embraced. It is the appropriate dynamic response to the gospel in the same way that the beggar's outstretched hand might be an appropriate way to receive the gold coin. Consequently, and this is the decisive point in this discussion of faith, Paul does not see the role of human faith as in any way undermining God's initiative and grace, but rather as establishing it.

> Therefore, the promise comes by faith, so that it may be by grace and may be guaranteed to all Abraham's offspring ... (Rom 4. 16a).

For Paul the fact that promise is received by faith means that salvation can be all of grace, that redemption is safeguarded as God's initiative, his decision, his act of mercy. For it is of the essence of faith to recognize that all is from God, and to exercise such faith is to affirm the freedom of God to be gracious according to his own volition. Faith flourishes in a context of total human helplessness and of the unlimited grace, mercy and power of God's love.

Conclusion

In seeking to understand the nature of faith in salvation I have argued that the following three principles are essential components of an adequate doctrine of justifying faith: faith is a gift of God; faith is the appropriate human response to the gospel; faith looks away from itself and towards God alone for salvation. If one of these elements is absent a doctrine of faith inevitably suffers serious distortion. In particular, I have shown why the theory that Jesus Christ believed in our stead leads to an unavoidable circularity and also fails to give an adequate account of the New Testament witness to the function of human faith. Abraham not Christ is the paradigm of justifying faith in the New Testament. Like Abraham we are called to trust in the promise of Christ.

I have also sought to show how these three principles can be held together in a coherent way. Paul's explication of faith as a dynamic trust in the divine promise allows faith to be considered as the appropriate human response to the gospel in a way which affirms the absolute sovereignty of God in salvation. For this sort of faith, by its nature, looks away from all human ability and finds its security in the total sufficiency of a gracious

God. Rather than undermining the efficacy of Christ's work such faith is wholly dependent on it. The three principles summarized above thus have a symbiotic relationship, they require one another. *Sola gratia* and *sola fides* rather than being alternative theological principles are mutually dependent in the *ordo salutis*.

But if faith is trust in the divine promise we need to consider more closely what that promise is and how our understanding of such a gospel impinges on our theory of the atonement.

6

The Gospel as Promise

I have argued from the Scriptures and the tradition that faith is the required human response to the proclamation of the gospel, where faith is to be understood principally as trusting in or appropriating the divine promise of salvation. Paul recognized that faith construed in this way allows salvation to be experienced as the secure gift of divine grace.

> Therefore, the promise comes by faith, so that it may be by grace and may be guaranteed to all Abraham's offspring ... (Rom 4. 16a).

Conversely, as might be expected, whenever the role of faith in salvation is neglected or misunderstood the gracious word of promise in Christian proclamation tends to be obscured or even lost and the appeal to its hearers becomes little more than a call for personal allegiance, transformation of life, or some other human endeavour. Hope is replaced by various forms of duty and the pearl of great price is neither recognized nor possessed.

The purpose of this chapter is to consider the nature and role of the divine promise that is disclosed in the gospel proclamation as we find it in the New Testament witness.

The kingdom of heaven as promise

Both John the Baptist and Jesus are reported as having begun their public ministry announcing to the people of Galilee and Judea the good news that the kingdom of God was soon to come. What is somewhat surprising is the nature of the general response to this message. It would appear that the people went down in droves from Jerusalem and the surrounding area to the Jordan Valley to repent openly of their sins and be baptized by John. Why, one might ask, did the message of the kingdom of heaven result in these widespread acts of penitence?

The gospel writers understood the ministry of John the Baptist as a fulfilment of the prophecy in Isaiah.

> A voice of one calling:
> 'In the desert prepare the way for the Lord;
> make straight in the wilderness a highway for our God.
> Every valley shall be raised up, every mountain and hill made low;
> the rough ground shall become level, the rugged places a plain.

And the glory of the Lord will be revealed.
and all mankind together will see it. For the mouth of the Lord has
spoken' ...

You who bring good tidings to Zion, go up on a high mountain.
You who bring good tidings to Jerusalem, lift up your voice with a shout,
Lift it up, do not be afraid; say to the towns of Judah, 'Here is your
God!' (Isa 40. 3–5, 9).

The announcement of the coming kingdom of God would have implied
to the Judaeans who heard John preaching that their divine king would
soon openly rule his people. Precisely what form this rule would take and
how it was related to contemporary Jewish expectation, whether national-
istic, apocalyptic or prophetic is a matter we can leave to one side for the
moment. Our present query is simply: 'Why was the announcement of this
coming rule of God not an occasion for general celebration? Why did it
lead to acts of public penitence?'

Let me, with the use of an historical paradigm, draw attention to a
concern that was likely to be raised by this message of the coming kingdom
of God. On 26 August 1944, General Charles de Gaulle led the Free French
Forces along the Champs-Elysées in a victory parade which celebrated the
liberation of Paris from the forces of German occupation. It was a day of
overflowing joy for the people of France after that great nation had been
forced to suffer four terrible years of humiliation under a foreign power.
The regime change which that day signified was, however, not welcome
news for every French citizen. Many of the leaders of the French (Vichy)
government were duly arrested and charged with high treason and other
crimes against the people. A number were executed and the prime minister,
Marshal Pétain, was fortunate to have his death sentence commuted to life
imprisonment. Thousands of ordinary citizens, who had collaborated with
the German authorities as spies and informers or had developed romantic
relationships with German soldiers, were to suffer public humiliation at the
hands of their fellow countrymen. In the years following the war a host of
dark truths were to emerge. It became clear that the Vichy government had
actively participated in the deportation of some seventy thousand Jews to
the German concentration camps and practised an anti-Semitism perhaps
even more virulent than that of the Italian Fascists. It was apparent that
a great number of ordinary French folk were complicit in these crimes
against humanity. The overthrow of German rule in France meant that
some had to face up to the consequence of their deeds immediately, while
countless others were destined to live on with shameful memories of their
actions during the years of occupation.

The coming of the rule of God was wonderful and liberating news for the
Jewish people who had lived for so long under foreign domination, but it
was so in a somewhat ambiguous way. On hearing the proclamation of the
kingdom of heaven many would have been aware that they too had been
complicit in the deeds of the various and complex dark powers that had

determined their lives. They would have been concerned that their actions would be brought to light under the rule of a God before whom no secrets remain hidden. And so it was that on learning of the imminent appearance of his kingdom large numbers of them made their way to the Jordan, using the opportunity provided to repent publicly and seek forgiveness for their sins. It was as though a general amnesty had been granted. The accounts we have all affirm this close link between the proclamation of the kingdom of heaven by John and Jesus and widespread acts of penitence by the general populace. In the Gospels of Matthew and Luke it is made clear that John was not satisfied with superficial indications of repentance from those who came to the Jordan to be baptized. He demanded indications of a trans-formation of life and attitude that bore testimony to the reality of their outward acts of contrition.

The canonical prophets had long since recognized that there was this element of ambiguity about the good news of the coming kingdom and challenged the complacent attitude with which many Jews looked forward to the day of God's appearing.

> Woe to you who long for the day of the Lord!
> Why do you long for the day of the Lord?
> That day will be darkness, not light.
> It will be as though a man fled from a lion only to meet a bear,
> as though he entered his house and rested his head on the wall
> only to have a snake bite him.
> Will not the day of the Lord be darkness not light –
> pitch dark, without a ray of brightness? (Amos 5. 18–20).

So too Jesus consistently cautions his hearers that the coming kingdom of heaven is not to be considered as unqualified good news. On that day there will be goats as well as sheep, tares along with the wheat, foolish virgins among the wise, good fish to be put in baskets and stale fish to be thrown away. For every Lazarus begging at the gate there is likely to be an uncon-cerned 'rich man' feeding sumptuously inside. Some who are forgiven will fail to forgive others; some who are invited to the banquet will make their excuses. As Albert Schweitzer so ably demonstrated,[61] there is an apocalyptic core to Jesus' proclamation of the kingdom which can not be domesticated within the comfortable and complacent religious world-view of nineteenth-century liber-alism. The dawning of God's kingdom in the sense of the open manifestation of his divine rule is good news to angels and to those who have no fear that their secret lives might be disclosed before the judge of all the earth. For the rest of us there is in it every reason for apprehension.

But the message of the coming kingdom is more than one of divine lordship, sovereign rule and final judgement. It is also the story of seed widely scattered, that will in certain favourable circumstances germinate, come to life and bear much fruit. It is a parable about a treasure of great

---

[61] Albert Schweitzer, *The Quest of the Historical Jesus* (London, SCM Press Ltd, 1981).

value discovered and possessed, or of a father's joy when a rebellious son returns home. It is a series of sermons about mercy and blessing for the humble folk of this world, for the poor in spirit, for those who mourn. It is the narrative of a servant who spent his life ministering among the sick, the sinful and the outcasts rather than among the upright and the well. It is the unexpected word of forgiveness to a paralytic borne on a stretcher by his faithful friends. It is testimony to a God who discloses himself to those whom one would least expect.

> At that time Jesus said, 'I praise you, Father, Lord of heaven and earth, because you have hidden these things from the wise and learned, and revealed them to little children. Yes, Father, for this was your good pleasure' (Matt 11. 25, 26).

Clothed in this presentation of the kingdom there is always some word of life, of hope, of grace, of mercy or of encouragement – a promise of peace: 'Come to me, all you who are weary or burdened, and I will give you rest' (Matt 11. 28). And it is as divine promise in this form that the kingdom of heaven is good news for all who are enabled to hear it. It becomes to them a precious pearl to be taken hold of, to be possessed, to be believed.

There are then these two somewhat different perspectives from which we can view the kingdom of God. First, it is the rule of God, the lordship of his Christ, the divine triumph over all the dark powers that have set themselves up against the high God of heaven. In it the forces of evil are overthrown and Jesus of Nazareth, the vicegerent of the Father, is exalted to a position of supreme lordship, from which he shall receive due obeisance from every person, principle and power. But, second, the kingdom of heaven is a word of gracious promise and the transformation it brings – a small seed that under particular conditions produces new life and bears fruit for eternity.

For those whose lives have been sullied by sin, the proclamation of the kingdom as divine rule can only be cause for deep concern, reason enough to repent and confess openly. But when the promise of grace is discovered in it, the kingdom of heaven is unqualified good news, to be gladly appropriated and wholeheartedly believed. And through the transforming power of its promise, the awesome message of the coming divine rule, by some strange irony, also becomes one of joy, great hope and glad expectation. With changed hearts the children of promise now find themselves delighting to honour and worship their true king. Nevertheless, the essence of the gospel is to be found not in the power, the rule, the lordship, the judgement or the coming glory of the kingdom, but in its quiet and often hidden word of gracious promise.

The apostolic preaching as promise

Not long before the Second World War, the New Testament scholar C. H. Dodd gave a series of lectures at King's College London which were published as *The Apostolic Preaching and its Developments.*[62] He argued for what he termed a 'realized' eschatology as the authentic perspective of the earliest Christian communities. But of particular significance to our present discussion was his view that the proclamation of the Aramaic-speaking Church at Jerusalem followed the basic pattern of the preaching of John the Baptist and Jesus.

> We may take it that this is what the author of Acts meant by 'preaching the Kingdom of God.' It is very significant that it follows the lines of the summary of the preaching of Jesus as given in Mark i. 14–15: 'Jesus came into Galilee preaching the Gospel of God, and saying, "the time is fulfilled, and the Kingdom of God has drawn near: repent and believe the Gospel".' This summary provides the framework within which the Jerusalem *kerygma* is set (p. 45).

Was Dodd right? Is Luke able to speak of the early evangelists proclaiming 'the kingdom of God'[63] because he believed their theme was continuous with the early ministry of Jesus? Let us briefly examine the opening chapters of the Acts of the Apostles. The sermons of Peter in Jerusalem, as Luke records them, are all occasioned by dramatic manifestations of the Holy Spirit and have as their central theme the resurrection of Jesus of Nazareth. This is the primary text: 'But God raised him from the dead,' and the implication of this divine action is that Jesus has been crowned as king – the people have a new sovereign. A descendant of David has ascended the throne (2. 30); and has been exalted to the right hand of God till all his enemies are made a footstool for his feet (2. 33–5). God has made him both Lord and Christ (2. 36). 'Anyone who does not listen to him will be completely cut off from among his people' (3. 23). ' ... he is the one whom God appointed as judge of the living and the dead' (10. 42b). It is not difficult to see why the announcement that Jesus has been inaugurated as king through his resurrection is continuous with the earlier proclamation by John the Baptist and Jesus that the Kingdom of God was at hand – that the King was coming.

It is also interesting that the proclamation of the resurrection was ambiguous good news in much the same way as that of the earlier preaching of the Kingdom of God. The death of Jesus is continually referred to in these sermons as an event for which the community was indirectly culpable: 'you with the help of wicked men put him to death'; 'you disowned the Holy and Righteous One and asked that a murderer be released to you'; 'and now you have betrayed and murdered him'. As we saw earlier, the exaltation of Jesus to a position of authority and rule was consequently a cause for deep concern to the hearers of the proclamation.

> When the people heard this, they were cut to the heart and said to Peter and the other apostles, 'Brothers, what shall we do?' (Acts 2. 37).

[62] C. H. Dodd, *The Apostolic Preaching and its Developments* (London, Hodder and Stoughton, 1936).
[63] Acts 8. 12; 14. 22; 19. 8; 28. 31.

The response of the evangelist closely parallels that which was given to the crowds in the Jordan valley. 'Repent and be baptized every one of you, in the name of Jesus Christ, so that your sins may be forgiven' (2. 38); '(r)epent then and turn to God, so that yours sins may be wiped out ... ' (3. 19); ' ... everyone who believes in him receives forgiveness of sins through his name' (10. 43b). The message of the resurrection of Jesus, like that of the coming kingdom, gave rise to great apprehension among those whose lives had been compromised by their complicity with sinful public action. Many who heard it availed themselves of the opportunity to repent and be baptized so that their sins might not be held against them by the high judge of heaven.

The content of the proclamation of the Apostles, as we have it in Acts, was of course more than the resurrection of Jesus to a position of honour, power and authority as judge of both the living and the dead. There was always within it a word of promise. Preaching to the people who had gathered in Solomon's Colonnade, Peter is recorded as concluding his sermon with these words:

> And you are heirs of the prophets and of the covenant God made with your fathers. He said to Abraham, 'Through your offspring all peoples on earth will be blessed.' When God raised up his servant, he sent him first to you to bless you by turning each of you from your wicked ways (3. 24, 25).

The promise once made to Abraham is now offered to those gathered in Jerusalem to hear Peter. All the blessings of that covenant are incorporated in Peter's word of grace. The proclamation is thus also one of promise and hope. Similarly, the record of Peter's sermon on the Day of Pentecost concludes with a clear word of promise. The great end-time blessing of God on the people of this world, both young and old, was recognized by the Church as being fulfilled in the gift of the Holy Spirit. In reponse to the plea for help from his troubled hearers Peter answers:

> Repent and be baptised every one of you in the name of Jesus Christ so that your sins may be forgiven. And you will receive the gift of the Holy Spirit. The promise is for you and your children and for all who are far off – for all whom the Lord our God will call (2. 38, 39).

The double-sided divine promise in Peter's proclamation entails the forgiveness of past sins and the creative new life of the Holy Spirit. The resurrection of Jesus Christ gives rise to the predicament before which the hearers find themselves. Through the transforming power of the promise this lordship of Christ becomes to the believers their hope, their duty and their proud confession. But the gospel as such, that which is good news for those whose lives are tarnished, lies not so much in the proclamation of resurrection but in the word of promise, the offer of forgiveness and of new life in the Spirit.

The covenant as promise

In his letter to the churches in Galatia Paul employs a number of arguments to buttress his interpretation of the gospel. One of these is derived from the institution of the Abrahamic covenant. The discussion is fairly straight-forward and needs minimal comment. The covenant with Abraham was founded on a promise that God gave to him and to his offspring (3. 16). ' … (T)he law introduced 430 years later, does not set aside the covenant previously established by God and thus do away with the promise' (v. 17). On the contrary, promise remains the basis for receiving the inheritance, or as we might say, for experiencing salvation. 'For if the inheritance depends on the law, then it no longer depends on the promise; but God in his grace gave it to Abraham through a promise' (v. 18). This does not mean that the law is to be regarded as in some way opposed to God's promise. Rather we are to understand the law as having a supervisory role until the time of Christ (v. 25). Paul goes on to use the figures of Sarah and Hagar as representations of the two covenants. 'For it is written that Abraham had two sons, one by the slave woman and the other by the free woman. His son by the slave woman was born in the ordinary way; but his son by the free woman was born as the result of promise. These may be taken figuratively for the women represent two covenants' (4. 22–4).

Why is the argument that the covenant with Abraham is founded on promise of such significance to Paul in his defence of the gospel? The idea of divine promise is for him firmly bound to a whole set of allied concepts. If salvation is the outcome of God's promise then it has the nature of divine gift rather than of human construction. It indicates a gospel that is dependent on divine mercy, determination and implementation rather than on human endeavour. Consequently, as to its administration, it is a gospel of grace rather than of law; as to our human response, it is a gospel of faith rather than of works; and its outcome in our experience is one of freedom rather than slavery; as we live according to the Spirit and not the flesh. Paul's underlying reasoning is a model of simplicity. The determin-ative covenant is based on a promise, which is to be received by faith, so that salvation might be all of grace, that is, all of God. By demonstrating that the covenant is founded on promise and not law, he has established the allied theses that salvation is to be appropriated by faith and not works and that it is derived wholly from God and not from human resources. And these three mutually dependent sets of ideas provide the parameters of the gospel that he has been commissioned to proclaim.

What was God's promise to Abraham? It was the promise of Isaac, a legit-imate son. This meant it was to him the hope of a future; his name would not be forever lost; he would receive the inheritance from God for which he longed. It was consequently for Abraham the promise of divine blessing, of salvation. It included the promise that through his offspring, understood by Paul as pointing to Christ, God would bless the world. It was consequently also a promise to us. Those who believe are considered by Paul as the true children of Abraham, the rightful heirs of this promise. His argument is that from the time that God first called a people to be his own, salvation has come by way of divine promise, received through faith, so that it might be wholly of grace.

Whereas Paul contrasts the covenant made with Abraham with that of Mount Sinai, the writer to the Hebrews draws a distinction between Jeremiah's 'new' covenant and the 'old' Mosaic covenant instituted in the desert. 'For if there had been nothing wrong with that first covenant, no place would have been sought for another. But God found fault with the people and said:

> The time is coming, declares the Lord, when I will make a new covenant with the house of Israel and with the house of Judah. It will not be like the covenant I made with their forefathers when I took them by the hand to lead them out of Egypt, because they did not remain faithful to my covenant, and I turned away from them, declares the Lord. This is the covenant I will make with the house of Israel after that time, declares the Lord. I will put my laws in their minds and write them on their hearts. I will be their God, and they will be my people ... For I will forgive their wickedness and will remember their sins no more.

By calling this covenant "new" he has made the first one obsolete, and what is obsolete and aging will soon disappear' (Heb 8. 7–10, 12, 13).

What is the promise on which this new covenant is based? It has two aspects. First, God will change the attitude of his people's hearts and minds so that they might love his law and walk joyfully in his ways. They will delight to serve him. Second, He will forgive their sins. All that is obnoxious in their lives he will put aside and absolve so that he might delight in them. And it is these two complementary promises that the writer recognizes as forming the basis of the hope of the people of the new covenant – divine forgiveness and the transformation of their hearts and minds. We see that the nature of the promise outlined here is remarkably similar to that found in the preaching of Peter as recorded in the Acts of the Apostles.

The content of the promise in the theology and preaching of Paul

If the idea of promise is central in the soteriology of Paul, what does he understand to be its content? What does he believe to be the essence of the good news or gospel that he is called to proclaim? It is, in short, the promise of righteousness.

> I am not ashamed of the gospel, because it is the power of God for the salvation of everyone who believes: first for the Jew then for the Gentile. For in the gospel a righteousness from God is revealed, a

righteousness that is by faith from first to last, just as it is written: 'The righteous will live by faith' (Rom 1. 16, 17).

In a world where many have chosen to worship the creature rather than the creator in open defiance of God's self-revelation; where moral inconsistency and hypocrisy are endemic in the lives of both the outwardly upright and the religious; where 'Jews and Gentiles are alike under sin', Paul's pessimistic conclusion is that '(t)here is no one righteous, not even one' (Rom 3. 9, 10). And to all these peoples, universally devoid of inherent righteousness, God in freedom and grace offers a new righteousness.

That this saving righteousness comes in the form of promise is seen first in the repeated and close conjunction that *dikaiosyne* (righteousness), along with its cognates, has with those of *pistis* (faith). 'This righteousness from God comes through faith in Jesus Christ for all who believe' (Rom 3. 22). 'Abraham believed God and it was credited to him as righteousness' (Rom 4. 3). 'We too have put our faith in Jesus Christ so that we may be justified (that is declared or made righteous) by faith in Christ and not by observing the law' (Gal 2. 16b). Faith for Paul is used in the main to indicate the appropriation of divine promise. Saving righteousness is for him the essence of that promise.

A remarkable feature of much current New Testament scholarship on the significance of the 'righteousness of' or 'from God' in Pauline thought is that the concept is often discussed and explicated with almost no reference to human faith, notwithstanding the prominence of the idea in the text. The failure to recognize the dynamic role of faith means, as was suggested at the start of the chapter, that the idea of promise in the proclamation tends to be obscured or even lost and the meaning of righteousness or justification is dislocated from a believing response to that promise.

Second, saving righteousness is made known to us through an act of divine disclosure. Paul speaks of this 'righteousness from God' as being revealed (Rom 1. 17) or being made manifest or known (Rom 3. 21). As promise, this righteousness from God is not a static, objective, universal reality, but the outcome of a dynamic relationship of disclosure, recognition and appropriation. It is a promise to be grasped by faith by those who recognize it for what it is. It is for eyes that have been opened to see, for ears that have been enabled to hear. That not everyone sees or hears was a matter that Paul found deeply disturbing, particularly as it related to many of his fellow Jews.

> For I can testify about them that they are zealous for God, but their zeal is not based on knowledge. Since they did not know the righteousness that comes from God and sought to establish their own, they did not submit to God's righteousness. Christ is the end of the law so that there may be righteousness for everyone who believes (Rom 10. 2, 3).

Third, that saving righteousness comes as promise is closely linked to the principle that redemption is wholly from God and not from human endeavour. If righteousness is received by way of divine promise it has the nature of gift and its source lies in God and not in ourselves. Earlier it was suggested that Paul's understanding of salvation was shaped by three sets of mutually dependent ideas: it is founded on promise and not law; it is appropriated by faith and not works; it is derived from God and not human resources. It is the third of these which finds particular emphasis in the phrase 'the righteousness of God' or more clearly 'the righteousness which comes from God'. For Paul the distinguishing feature of such right-eousness is that it is not a humanly contrived condition. It is of God and not of ourselves, a contrast that he stresses.

> I consider them rubbish, that I may gain Christ and be found in him, not having a righteousness of my own that comes from the law, but that which is through faith in Christ – that righteousness that comes from God and is by faith (Phil 3. 8b, 9).

This is the heart of Paul's gospel. Although the three sets of ideas imply one another, it seems to me that his insistence that salvation is by faith and not works and is founded on promise and not law, serve as supporting pillars for his central concern that our redemption be recognized as being wholly of God rather than as some form of human construct. He is quite unwilling to allow even the slightest ground for human arrogance. Rather, 'Let him who boasts, boast in the Lord' (see Rom 3. 27, 1 Cor 1. 26–31).

In this discussion I have taken the 'righteousness of God' to be a genitive of origin, a righteousness which comes from God, rather than a subjective genitive, describing either God's character or action. Such an interpretation is shared by Augustine[64] and Luther[65] and consequently is embedded in both Catholic and Protestant traditions. It is one, however, which recent scholarly opinion has tended to oppose. Among the English speaking theologians we have been considering, E. P. Sanders has argued that '*dikaiosyne theou* is the redemptive action of God, not a description of God's essence, nor of man's essence before God.'[66] N. T. Wright has helped popularize the view that it refers principally to God's covenant faithfulness.[67]

The difficulty, however, with interpreting *dikaiosyne theou* as covenant faithfulness is that the expectation that God will be faithful to his covenant with Israel is precisely what Paul does not want to emphasize at this point

---

[64] 'This righteousness of God, which is the gift of grace without merits, is not known by those who go about to establish their own righteousness, and are therefore not subject to the righteousness of God, which is Christ.' Augustine, *City of God,* The Nicene and Post-Nicene Fathers (vol. VI–02) XXI, 24.

[65] 'Only the Gospel reveals the righteousness of God, that is, who is righteous, or how a person becomes righteous before God, namely, alone by faith, which trusts the Word of God.' Martin Luther, *Commentary on the Epistle to the Romans,* trans. by J. Theodore Mueller, (Grand Rapids, Zondervan Publishing House, 1954), p. 25.

[66] E. P. Sanders, *Paul and Palestinian Judaism* (Minneapolis, Fortress Press, 1977), p. 540.

[67] ' … to see the quality in question as God's faithfulness to his promises, to his covenant.' Tom Wright, *What St Paul Really Said* (Oxford, Lion Publishing plc, 1997), p. 102.

in his exposition (i.e. Rom 3. 21). To affirm the sense of security that Jews already felt in their perceived special relation with God would undermine Paul's argument in the first few chapters of Romans, where he is intent on showing that both Jews and Gentiles alike are together guilty and without excuse before God. Standing in the dock before God the Jews have no special privileges, they cannot look to God for any favoured relation. To say at this point that God is faithful to his covenant commitments would give a false sense of privilege to those who understood themselves to be children of the covenant. Consequently, Wright is compelled to widen his interpretation of the concept so that that it also indicates God's judicial role as the one who restores the world's broken order and points to his apocalyptic intervention in the end times as creator and judge of the world.[68] However, qualifying the term in this way brings its own difficulties. 'Covenant faithfulness' is now a rather complex concept that paradoxically does not imply any salvific privilege for the Jews. No evidence is offered indicating that first-century Jews or Gentiles would have generally understood it in this highly nuanced form. And if Paul is using the idea of covenant faithfulness with a quite new meaning, why does he not explain it, here or elsewhere? Why should this, what Wright considers as the central idea of his letter to the Romans, remain wholly undeveloped? It is far better, it seems to me, to apply Ockham's razor to the matter and take the simpler option. Having spent two chapters highlighting the failure of human righteousness, Paul refers in the third chapter of Romans to the revelation of a different order or type of righteousness, one that has God as its source and comes to the believer who has faith in Christ.

I have argued then that the promise of the gospel for Paul is of a righteousness that is derived from God. He is the one that makes, declares or constitutes us as righteous. It is he who justifies us. Since we have been justified by faith, we now have peace with him. But what of the process of sanctification, the transformation of our lives? What is the relation between the new righteousness of Christians and their holiness, between justification and sanctification? In Paul the two are bound together not through a natural relation, whereby one structurally includes the other, but through the loving decision of God.

> Since we have now been justified by his blood, how much more shall we be saved from God's wrath through him! For if when we were God's enemies, we were reconciled to him through the death of his Son, how much more having been reconciled, shall we be saved through his life! (Rom 5. 9, 10).

The transformation of life and attitude whereby the Christian is enabled to complete the course and hold on to the faith is itself an act of God. The

[68] N. T. Wright, *The Letter to the Romans: Introduction, Commentary and Reflection*, The New Interpreter's Bible, A Commentary in Twelve Volumes, vol. X (Nashville, Abingdon Press, 2002), pp. 398–401.

God who declares his people to be righteous will himself bring them to glory. Having justified them through the death of his Son while they were enemies, now that they are reconciled, he will surely give to them all that is required to ensure that they are never separated from his love. Again we see that the promise has a twofold character. For Paul it is in the first place peace with God through divine justification, the promise of right-eousness. Secondly, it is a transformation of the person through the Spirit by participation in Christ's death and resurrection, an unfolding process of change that will lead to final glory. It is a radically different way of life, a new creation. It is the promise of regeneration.

The promise of the Son

In a variety of ways the Gospel writers seek to substantiate the claim that Jesus of Nazareth is the Christ, the anointed one, promised by God through the prophets to deliver his people from bondage. The geneal-ogies, the birth narratives, the miracles and exorcisms, the confession of Peter, the voice from heaven, the cries of those waving palm branches, Jesus' enigmatic response under interrogation, the events surrounding his crucifixion and resurrection, are all used to persuade the reader that this charismatic young teacher and healer from Galilee is none other than the long-expected Messiah of God. Why was it of such importance to the Early Church to demonstrate that Jesus was indeed the Christ of prophetic promise?

First, it places Jesus at the centre of God's gracious purpose for Israel and the world. The salvation of God for which pious Jews had waited patiently was to be found not in the political upheavals soon to befall their country, nor in the programmes of the competing religious parties within Judaism, but through the person and history of this one man. To behold him, it was held, even when he was but a child, was to behold the true hope of Israel.

Second, the identification of Jesus as God's Messiah inextricably links his person with the advent, the promise and the authority of the Kingdom of Heaven. The early Christians came to believe that through Jesus' teaching, healings and mighty works the kingdom of God had already been manifest in their midst; that his sufferings and cruel death were the ordained path which, in obedience to his Father, he chose to tread so as to bring about the promise of the kingdom; and that through his resurrection he had been exalted to a place of sovereign authority over it, so that it might be divinely administered through him. 'The Lord God will give him the throne of his father David, and he will reign over the house of Jacob forever, his kingdom will never end' (Luke 1. 32b, 33). If Jesus is indeed the Christ of God it means that all the promises of the Kingdom of Heaven come to fulfilment in his person and ministry.

Similarly, we find that the promise underlying the concept of divine covenant is also firmly wedded in New Testament thought to the person of

Jesus. This is clearly indicated in the words of the Eucharist: 'In the same way, after the supper, he took the cup saying, "This cup is the new covenant in my blood which is poured out for you"' (Luke 22. 20). Jesus' passion was recognized by the Church as the foundation of the new covenant with its promises of forgiveness and transformation. So too it is apparent that Paul's understanding of the promise of the gospel in terms of 'the righteousness of God' is wholly dependent on the redemption or atonement effected through Christ's sacrificial death and his resurrection to a place of intercession at the right hand of the Father (see Rom 3. 24, 25; 4. 25; 8. 34).

In short, all the promises of God disclosed in the proclamation of the gospel, as we have considered them in the above discussion, find their fulfilment in the person and ministry of Jesus. In Paul's words: 'For no matter how many promises God has made, they are "Yes" in Christ' (2 Cor 1. 20). Jesus is, we might say, the treasure-chest of all his gracious promises to us. He is in effect the content of God's pledge to the world.

In the Scriptures this concept of Jesus as the embodiment of the divine promise of salvation finds its most articulate expression in a number of phrases of the form: 'God gave his only Son for us'.

> He who did not spare his own Son, but gave him up for us all – how will he not also, along with him, graciously give us all things? (Rom 8. 32)?
>
> He sent his one and only Son into the world that we might live through him. This is love: not that we loved God, but that he loved us and sent his Son as an atoning sacrifice for our sins (1 John 4. 9, 10).
>
> For God so loved the world that he gave his one and only Son, that whoever believes in him shall not perish but have eternal life (1 John 3. 16).

The richness of theological meaning that comes to expression in these summary statements of the Christian gospel has long been recognized by the community of faith. A consideration of the phraseology used in them suggests that all three texts are in some measure dependent on the narrative of Abraham's journey to Moriah to sacrifice Isaac.

> Then God said, 'Take your son, your only son Isaac, whom you love, and go to the region of Moriah. Sacrifice him there as a burnt offering on one of the mountains I will tell you about' (Gen 22. 2).

What then are the key theological features of these passages?

1. There is a clear indication in them of both the enormity and costliness of God's love towards us.
2. The unique relation of the Son to the Father, along with the suggestion of loss to the Father in giving him over, are clear pointers to the Son's divine status.
3. The gift of his Son is the embodiment of all that God would give or promise to his people.

4. The giving of the Son implies that he is given over to death.
5. The purpose of the gift of the Son is so that we might have life and not perish under God's righteous judgement.
6. The Son is given for us; he dies so that we might not die; he is given in our place or stead.

Having in mind the theological comprehensiveness of the themes suggested by the idea of the Son as divine gift, the following short summary is offered of the various promises that form the content of the New Testament gospel proclamation:

God gave his Son for us.

The promise of the Holy Spirit

We have seen in the discussion above that there is a pattern to the promises disclosed in the gospel proclamation of the first Christians. The promise of salvation generally has two aspects. On the one hand there is in it the offer of forgiveness or peace with God, on the other there is the pledge of spiritual renewal and transformation of life.

The major focus of this work has been on the atonement, understood in terms of reconciliation or peace with God accomplished through the life, death and resurrection of Christ. This limitation of the project's scope, however, is not meant to detract from the significance of the divine promise to renew and transform those whom God has redeemed. The promise of the gospel is not only one of forgiveness, but also of cleansing from unrighteousness. It offers not merely peace but spiritual life. Participation in Christ means not only our justification, but also a sharing in his death and resurrection. It has to do with sanctification and the preparation for glory.

It is helpful to describe God's project among us as a renewal of the divine image in the church. The likeness of God which was lost by humankind in antiquity is now to be re-formed among God's people after the pattern of Jesus. And this task is the particular work of the Holy Spirit.

It is by the Spirit that our eyes are opened to recognize the glory of God in the face of Christ; it is by the Spirit that we are drawn to the promise of the gospel and are made willing to take hold of it. But it is also by the Spirit that we learn to delight in God, to love him and follow his ways faithfully, for the Spirit softens our calloused hearts and writes God's law upon them. It is the Spirit who enables us to pray, worship and to cry out to God as our Father. The new characteristics of love, peace, patience and kindness are just some of the many fruits of God's Spirit in a Christian life that enable us, through our conformity to the life of Jesus, to bear again the divine image in the world and to serve its people. In short, the second great promise of the gospel is dependent on the first and can be summarized in a similar manner.

God gives his Spirit to us.

The self-offering of God

One expression figures repeatedly in the divine declarations of covenant promise as they are recorded in the Scriptures.

> I will establish my covenant as an everlasting covenant between me and you and your descendants after you for the generations to come, *to be your God* and the God of your descendants after you (Gen 17. 17).
>
> 'This is the covenant I will make with the house of Israel after that time,' declares the Lord. 'I will put my laws in their minds and write it on their hearts. *I will be their God and they will be my people.*' (Jer 31. 31, see also Ezek 36. 28, Heb 8. 10).
>
> I will say to those called 'Not my people,' '*You are my people*'; and they will say, '*You are my God*' (Hos 2. 22b).
>
> And I heard a loud voice from heaven saying, 'Now the dwelling of God is with men, and he will live with them. *They will be his people, and God himself will be with them and be their God* (Rev 21. 3).

In both Testaments it is apparent that all the good that is to be ours in time and eternity is recognized as flowing from the river of this primal promise that God himself will be our God even as we shall be his people. He will in love be faithful to us eternally; he will ensure that we continue to love him in faithfulness. The gift of the Son for us and that of the Spirit to us are the two great streams that derive from this, the ultimate promise that God makes of himself to be our God.[69]

Conclusion

We have found in the various strands of gospel proclamation in the New Testament a revelation of divine promise. The good news of the Kingdom of Heaven is to be discovered not so much in its power or authority but in its words of hope to those who are unworthy of it. Likewise in the preaching of the Jerusalem church as recorded in Acts, the gospel lies not principally in the announcement of the resurrection of Jesus but in the promise of forgiveness and of the Holy Spirit to the penitent. For Paul the gospel is understood in terms of the promise of a new righteousness for the ungodly. I have argued that the inner logic of New Testament thought leads one to summarize these various aspects of gospel promise in the following trinitarian form:

---

[69] For this analysis I am much indebted to the writing of the Puritan, John Owen, see *A Discourse concerning the Holy Spirit,* vol. III, p. 23 and *The Doctrine of the Saints' Perseverance Explained and Confirmed,* vol. 11 in The Works of John Owen, ed. by William H Goold (London, Banner of Truth Trust, 1965–8), p. 232.

God gave his Son for us and gives his Spirit to us so that he might eternally be our God even as we are to be his people.

The gospel is no more and no less than the proclamation of this divine promise.

This is the content of the pledge of divine love made to the unworthy and is to be received or appropriated by faith. As it is ultimately God's gift of himself to us, it is indivisible. Although in Christian proclamation the presentation of the gospel, along with our belief, is always partial and incomplete, nevertheless, to receive even the smallest element of God's gracious promise to us, is to become heir of all that he offers of himself through his Son and by his Spirit.

We should not be deceived by the simplicity of the statement above relating the gospel to the divine promise for it has within itself the power to turn much of modern soteriological thought on its head.

7

The Way of Salvation

Our focus in the last two chapters has been on the content and form of the good news proclaimed by the first Christians and the nature of the response required of those who heard it. I have argued that the content is some aspect of the comprehensive, trinitarian pledge that God makes of himself, in love, through the gift of both his Son and his Spirit. The form is that of a promise which is to be received or taken hold of in faith.

There is, what one might call, a symbiotic relation between these ideas of promise and faith as they are used in the New Testament, in that they depend on one another for their efficacy. The significance or value of faith does not lie in itself as a human virtue or even as divine gift, but rather in the content of that which it grasps – the promise of God. Similarly, the power of the gospel promise comes to expression only through the exercise of faith. In the New Testament the blessings of the Kingdom of Heaven invariably refer to those who believe.

Let us, then, consider more closely this Spirit-animated dynamic of gospel promise and responsive faith to which the Scriptures bear such clear witness. What role or function does it play in the way of salvation? Do the New Testament authors understand it as the means used by God to effect salvation or is it to be viewed as something rather less crucial in the redemptive process? Is the preaching of the good news the means by which God saves those who believe or does he use it simply to assure them that they have already been reconciled through the death of his Son? Is the gift of a responsive faith instrumental in our redemption or is it no more than an indicator that we are indeed the children of Abraham, the people of God? It is necessary to proceed carefully here for these are important issues and, as we shall see, much turns upon them.

Paul, along with other New Testament authors, recognizes that a believing response to the proclamation of the gospel is a reliable indicator or manifestation of God's hidden electing purposes:[70]

> For we know, brothers and sisters loved by God, that he has chosen you, because our gospel came to you not simply with words, but also with power, with the Holy Spirit and with deep conviction (1Thess 1. 4, 5a).

Prior to any response that we might make to God, stands the choice that God has already made of us.[71] In that sense our Spirit-enabled reception

---

[70] See Acts 13. 48.
[71] See also Matt 11. 25–7; John 6. 65; 15. 16; 1 Pet 1, 2.

of the good news is a manifestation of the hidden, sovereign and loving purpose of God to draw us to himself. Nevertheless the dynamic of gospel promise and responsive faith, in Paul's thought, functions as far more than an indicator of these foundational realities. He was convinced that preaching the message of the atonement is used by God to *effect* the salvation of those who believe.

> For Christ did not send me to baptise, but to preach the gospel – not with wisdom and eloquence, lest the cross of Christ be emptied of its power. For the message of the cross is foolishness to those who are perishing, but to us who are being saved it is the power of God. For since in the wisdom of God the world through its wisdom did not know him, God was pleased through the foolishness of what was preached to save those who believe (1 Cor 1. 17, 18, 21).

This view that the gospel promise, responded to in faith, is salvific is widely attested in the New Testament. It is suggested in Jesus' parables about the sowing of seed; it is indicated in all those texts which directly relate faith in the message of Christ's death and resurrection with forgiveness, justification or salvation; it is implied in the dire warnings of judgement given to those who do not respond to the message of the gospel with faith;[72] it is the reason why the role of the preacher of the good news is considered to be indispensable.

> 'Everyone who calls on the name of the Lord will be saved.' How, then, can they call on the one they have not believed in? And how can they believe in the one of whom they have not heard? And how can they hear without someone preaching to them? And how can they preach unless they are sent? As it is written, 'How beautiful are the feet of those who bring good news!' Consequently, faith comes from hearing the message, and the message is heard through the word of Christ (Rom 10. 13–15, 17).

The biblical witness indicates that although God in his absolute freedom is the sovereign author of every aspect of our salvation, he accomplishes his redemptive purposes for our lives by means of the proclamation of the good news and our responsive faith to it. In short, the experience of reconciliation is dependent on hearing and believing the gospel. By the hidden working of his Spirit, it engenders faith in God's people, and that faith in turn appropriates the saving promise which forms its content.

Such an account of the way of salvation can hold its own in the face of persuasive competing theories? Karl Barth has been particularly effective in shaping the way many of us understand this process. Let us consider his argument.

---

[72] See Heb 2. 1, 2; 4. 1, 2; Luke 10. 8–12; Acts 13. 46.

The *ordo salutis* in Karl Barth

Barth explains the significance of the death of Christ within a mediatorial framework, one which has, by and large, been taken up in the argument of this book.

> And in his [the sinner's] place Jesus Christ rendered that obedience which is required of the covenant partner of God, and in that way found His good pleasure. He did it by taking to Himself the sins of all men, by suffering as His death the death to which they had fallen a prey, by freely offering Himself as the sacrifice which had to be made when God vindicated Himself in relation to man, by choosing to suffer the wrath of God in His own body and the fire of His love in His own soul[73] (IV. 1. pp. 94ff).

The vicarious death and resurrection of Christ is the basis of the righteous judgement of God, the divine pronouncement of pardon or justification of the guilty. We come then to our particular area of concern. How does Barth understand the relation of human faith to this divine declaration?

> The truth and power of faith depend on the fact that it is not a work of human arbitrariness, not even the arbitrariness of a supreme need and longing for redemption, but man's subjection to the divine verdict in which it is a matter of God's own honour and glory – and as such a subjection an act of pure obedience (IV. 1. p. 96).

Faith is not an arbitrary or independent activity. It is, rather, our obedient response to the divine verdict. But, and here is the important point, unbelief can not undo that verdict or alter its outcome. The judgement of God is universally valid whether or not those upon whom it is pronounced exercise any faith at all.

> Pardon – by God and therefore unconditionally pronounced and unconditionally valid – that is man's justification. In the judgement of God, according to His election and rejection, there is made in the midst of time, and as the central event of all human history, referring to all the men who live both before and after, a decision, a divisive sentence. Its result – expressed in the death and resurrection of Jesus Christ – is the pardon of man ... Whether man hears it, whether he accepts it and lives as one who is pardoned is another question (IV. 1. p. 568).

Christians are those who by the exercise of their faith realize they are saved. Faith has to do with the assurance of salvation, rather than its appropriation. 'It is in faith that man can find and know that he is justified with an ultimate confidence and assurance' (IV. 1. p. 96). But, and here Barth

---

[73] The reference is to Karl Barth, *Church Dogmatics,* vol. 4 part 1, ed. by G. W. Bromiley & T. F. Torrance (Edinburgh, T&T Clark, 1985), 4.1, p. 358.

is quite clear, the lack of such faith in no way undermines the reality of the salvation accomplished by God. ' … objectively, all are justified, sanctified and called' (IV. 1, p. 148), they simply don't know it or live in the light of it. They lack the assurance of faith. 'Faith of this kind is the work of the Holy Spirit which makes man a Christian' (IV. 1. p. 99). But, and this is significant, the Spirit is not given to all.

> ' … it is the Holy Spirit, the being and work of the one eternal God in this special form, that is still lacking in the world at large. That God did not owe His Son, and in that Son Himself, to the world, is revealed by the fact that He gives His Spirit to whom He will' (IV. 1, p. 148).

How are we to assess this account of the way of salvation? There is clearly much about it that is attractive. It emphasizes that salvation is a divine gift rather than a human achievement. It does much to remove 'the scandal of particularity' from Christian proclamation, for the preaching of the cross can not be of final significance to the world if the 'ultimate' issues of divine pardon, justification and sanctification have already been universally accomplished for everyone, whether or not they get to hear about them, or respond to him. It also lifts the burden of concern from those who might be anxious about their standing before God.

The problem, however, with Barth's conclusions is that they are simply not true. The idea that God has justified or pardoned all people of all time is clearly opposed to the biblical testimony and fails theologically. The New Testament witnesses have no knowledge of a salvation that is not worked out in the believer's life through the regenerating and transforming power of the Holy Spirit. Justification can not be isolated from incorporation into the death and life of Christ, with its liberation from the dominance of the addictions, fears and cravings of a sinful nature and entry into a new mode of being energized by the Holy Spirit. Those who have righteousness imputed to them will, like Abraham, manifest God's justifying declaration in an attitude of faithful obedience towards God. As James reminds us in his epistle, the one is manifest in the exercise of the other. Pardon of sins past is not to be separated from the process of divine deliverance from the present power of indwelling sin. Those who confess their shortcomings, God promises not only to forgive but to cleanse from all unrighteousness. It is a false and dangerous hope to offer those who continue to sin gladly and wantonly that God has nevertheless unconditionally pardoned them of their wrongs (see 1 John). Sanctification is a process of separation to God of which the recipients are not left unaware. Rather, their eyes need to be opened by the Spirit to behold the glory of the Lord and their hearts made willing to share in the sufferings of his mission if they are to be transformed into the likeness of Christ.

The theory that everyone is justified but only Christians receive the Spirit requires a radical disjunction between the salvation procured by the obedience, death and resurrection of Christ and its application in a believer's life through the working of the Holy Spirit; between the promised gift of God's Son to us and that of his Spirit for us.[74] Ultimately it implies a breach in the triune being of God. For is not the essence of all the covenantal promises that God will be our God? And does he not do so by graciously giving all of himself – Father, Son and Holy Spirit – to us?

In short, the proclamation of the gospel, as we find it in the New Testament, does not entail an indiscriminate declaration to its hearers that they have been unconditionally pardoned, reconciled or justified.

Barth's conclusions are derived in part from his understanding of the nature of the gospel as a divine verdict that is to be obeyed. This perception of the gospel as a sovereign decree or decision before which submission is required, is closely related to his argument that the essential content of revelation is that God is the Lord.

> We may sum all this up in the statement that God reveals Himself as the Lord. This statement is to be regarded as an analytical judgment. The distinction between form and content cannot be applied to the biblical concept of revelation. When revelation is an event according to the Bible, there is no second question as to what its content might be ... Without revelation man does not know that there is a Lord, that he, man, has a Lord, and that God is this Lord (I. 1, p. 306).

God is the Lord, and as the Lord he has made a sovereign, universal, unconditional verdict of justification of humankind whose truth is wholly independent of the whim or fancy of the creature. What is required of us is the obedience of faith, through which we are enabled to recognize and so live in the light of our new being in Christ.

There are a number of reasons why this model of Christian proclamation as 'a divine verdict to be obeyed' is problematic for theology. First, it detaches the efficacy of the word of proclamation from our human response; it severs the promise from faith. In the Scriptures the pledge of God's only Son promises life to those who believe, justification and faith are welded together; whereas in Barth's model the proclamation is able to stand on its own, it is effective quite apart from the response of the hearer. Second, it distorts our understanding of the nature of faith: for faith is not primarily obedience, although it leads to it; nor is it simply knowledge, although it entails it. Faith is rather a receiving of the promise; a grasping of the gift; a taking hold of Christ and all his benefits. Third, the message of good news is more than a declaration, command or verdict – it is a pledge of mercy and grace; it is not so much the decree of a sovereign ruler as it is the promise of a loving parent. Fourth, the function of the gospel as it is received in faith is not simply the means by which we come to know of our salvation, it is rather the instrument through which God in his freedom has chosen to reconcile to himself those who believe.

---

[74] Note: 'If anyone does not have the Spirit of Christ, he does not belong to Christ' (Rom 8. 9b).

Reconciliation accomplished and applied

The excursion we have taken into the working of faith and the place of promise in Early Christian preaching has this as its particular purpose: to establish that the dynamic of divine promise and responsive faith is an integral element in the process of salvation. In the words of Augustine: 'He who made you without your cooperation will not save you without it' (Sermons 169, 13). This dynamic of divine word and human response is sometimes referred to in the New Testament as God's call, for the biblical concept of invitation or call contains within itself the idea of promise.

> Come, all you who are thirsty, come to the waters;
> and you who have no money, come, buy and eat!
> Come, buy wine and milk without money and without cost (Isa 55. 1).

> Come to me, all who are weary and burdened, and I will give you rest. Take my yoke upon you and learn from me, for I am gentle and humble in heart and you will find rest for your souls. For my yoke is easy and my burden is light (Matt 11. 28–30).

And this divine call is effective in our lives when God not only makes a promise to us through what might be described as the public or external message of the gospel, but opens our ears so that we might hear it and gives us a heart to believe it. It is such a 'call' that Paul refers to in his outline of the way of salvation.

> And those he predestined, he also called; and those he called, he also justified; those he justified he also glorified (Rom 8. 30).

Now if God's call is a vital aspect of this redemptive process, how are we to understand the relation between the atonement accomplished through the life, death and resurrection of Jesus and that which is effected by the response of faith to the proclamation of the gospel? There is much to commend the simplicity of the proposal used in the sixteenth century soteriological discussion, which can take the following form:[75]

> The atonement procured through the ministry of Jesus Christ is brought to fruition, or made effective, in a believer's life through the work of the Holy Spirit.

Such a portrayal of their relationship makes it clear that the effectiveness of the Spirit's reconciling ministry through promise and faith is wholly dependent on what Christ has done and is doing: his self-offering and inter-cession. Consequently, the message of the gospel is not a random promise of divine deliverance but rather God's pledge to us on the basis of the atoning action of his Son. We can expect the content of that message to be wholly determined by the nature of Christ's reconciling ministry. Conversely, our

---

[75] Calvin heads the first section of his Third Book of the Institutes: 'The benefits of Christ made available to us by the secret operation of the Spirit.'

interpretation of the atonement is bound to be informed or illuminated by our understanding of the gospel. There is then, what we might call, a semiotic relationship between the shape and content of the gospel and the nature of the atonement: they serve to interpret one another.

What then is the gospel? We have argued that it takes the form of a gracious promise that God makes to the world, whose content, however partially it might be expressed or understood, is that God himself will be our God and we his people. There are two dimensions to this divine act of self-giving: God gives his Son for us and His Spirit to us. Such an understanding of the proclamation would indicate that the essence of the atonement is that Christ is given for us, even as he freely offers up himself on our behalf, that we might have peace with God. The Spirit is given that we might enter that promised world of fellowship with God, procured by the Son, and as his transformed people enjoy him for ever as we live for his glory in this world and the next. This is what we mean by a mediatorial theory of atonement. It is, as the reader will recognize, the substance of our thesis and to defend it is the purpose for which each argument of this book has been brought in to serve.

We have seen then that a mediatorial interpretation of the atonement throws light on, even as it is illuminated by, our understanding of the gospel as promise. The one gives support to the truth of the other. In so doing they satisfy an important test of theological adequacy – does the doctrine hang well with adjacent theological themes, does it play a coherent role in the 'rule of faith'?

There is, however, an alternative understanding of the gospel which views it, not in terms of promise and faith, but as a sovereign declaration, or divine demand, requiring our obedience. Such a view generally depends on a more triumphalist account of the atonement, one which has been designated earlier as the 'victory' model. These two interpretative theories also cohere well together. What we need to ask of them is whether they are able to give an adequate account of the material before them? If they do, my central argument, that mediation provides a normative interpretation of the atonement, is shown to be false.

Let us then consider a modern and popular form of this interpretation of the gospel and the atonement. It will also serve as a foil for the further development of our lines of thought as they are drawn to a conclusion.

The *ordo salutis* in Tom Wright

Tom Wright holds that the gospel, as we find the term used by Paul, is the proclamation of the divine lordship of Christ. In his book *What St Paul Really Said*, he says of the first chapter of Romans:

> Paul is explaining why he is eager to announce the gospel, the royal proclamation of King Jesus as Lord of the world, throughout the world and particularly at Rome itself ... Over against all the powers

of the world, not least those in Rome itself, the true God is revealed
as the one Lord of all the earth. And Paul is not ashamed to say so
(pp. 109ff).

For him the essence of the gospel is found in Rom 1. 2–4, particularly in the
phrase 'who through the Spirit of holiness was appointed the Son of God
in power through his resurrection from the dead'.

> Generations of scholars, determined to resist the idea that Paul
> thought of Jesus in any way as the king, the Messiah, the true Son
> of David, have of course allowed this passage to drop off the front
> of Romans, as they hurried on to what they took to be the real
> introductory formula in verses 16-17, the announcement of the right-
> eousness of God ... (pp. 52ff).

Breaking with this tradition, Wright champions what he calls the 'royal
theology of Paul' by showing that there is a link between the concept of
'good news' and that of divine kingship in Isaiah 40 and 52 (p. 42) and
also from the way the Greek term *euaggelion* or 'good news' was used in
relation to the emperors of the Roman world. The gospel is then for him
the proclamation of the kingship of Christ; it is the 'announcement about
the true God as opposed to the false gods' (p. 59).

Wright holds that the proclamation of this gospel is itself effective in salvation.
'The royal proclamation is not simply the conveying of true information about
the kingship of Jesus. It is the putting into effect of that kingship, the decisive
and authoritative summoning to allegiance' (p. 61). The required human
response to the message of this gospel, the rule of Christ, is our obedience.

> The proclamation is an authoritative summons to obedience – in
> Paul's case, to what he calls 'the obedience of faith' (p. 45).

Wright is quite clear that in this process 'faith' is not to be regarded as an
instrument of salvation in any way. It is rather a marker which indicates
membership of God's people. ' "Faith", for Paul, is therefore not a substitute
"work" in a moralistic sense. It is not something one does in order to gain
admittance in the covenant people. It is the badge that proclaims that one
is already a member.' (p. 132) '[It is] ... not something someone "performs"
as a kind of initiation test.' (p. 125).

This understanding of the gospel as the proclamation of divine lordship
demanding a response of obedience and allegiance corresponds with his
interpretation of the atonement as the divine victory over the false gods, sin
and death.

> The cross is for Paul the symbol, as it was the means, of the liberating
> victory of the one true God, the creator of the world, over all the
> enslaving powers that have usurped his authority (p. 47). Instead of a
> great military victory over Rome, Jesus as the representative Israelite
> had won a great victory over sin and death, the real enemies of the
> people of God and of the whole world (p. 93).

What do we make of such a portrayal of the way of salvation? Its structure is attractively simple. Shaped by a small, integrated set of ideas relating to governance (including those of authority, power, victory, order, allegiance and obedience), it is able to avoid a number of classical theological dilemmas that we might find in a soteriology ordered by a broader range of concepts.[76] Wright's somewhat militaristic matrix of controlling ideas provides an alternative interpretative scheme, a particular way of approaching the biblical material about salvation, one which is shaped by questions of governance. In so doing, it replaces a hermeneutical scheme that has tended to focus mainly on relationships, more specifically – how they are constituted, broken and restored. The question being considered here is whether Wright's 'way of salvation' gives an adequate interpretation of the material before it? My contention is that it fails to do so in three important areas of his thought.

Covenant

First, consider how Wright describes the purpose of the covenant:

> The covenant was there to put the world to rights, to deal with evil and to restore God's justice and order to the cosmos (p. 117).

But is this correct? Is the covenant simply a tool to bring order to a recalcitrant world? Is it merely a mechanism to overpower the opposition of evil? The covenant is about a divine promise, as Wright acknowledges.[77] At its core is the pledge that God makes first to Abraham and his offspring, but which we now understand includes us the Gentiles: 'I will be your God and you shall be my people.' It is an institution through which God might love us and we might love him. Within the covenant, the sacrificial system has a twofold purpose: to restore the unfaithful to fellowship with God and to enrich the fellowship of the faithful. From start to finish the covenant is all about relationships.

The covenant with Abraham includes the promise that through his seed God would bless the world. Out of this aspect of the promise Wright develops the theory that Israel saw herself as the creator's true humanity and so 'the creator's means of dealing with the sin of Adam, and hence with the evil of the world'.[78] This interesting but somewhat speculative theory then becomes for Wright the central purpose of the covenant. That which was considered as the basis and setting of our relationship with God now finds its primary significance as a divine agent of law

---

[76] Wright sees his system as eliminating the age-old difficulty of resolving divine justice and love. 'If you understand *dikaiosyne theou* in the way I have suggested, you cannot play off justice and love against one another.' *What St Paul Really Said* (p. 110).

[77] 'The basis of the covenant was of course the set of promises to the patriarchs ... ' N. T. Wright, *The New Testament and the People of God* (Minneapolis, Fortress Press, 1992) p. 260.

[78] N. T. Wright, *op. cit.*, p. 262.

enforcement. 'It is there to put the world to rights.' It is as though we were to redefine marriage as a means to keep difficult children in order. It has in it an element of truth but it is surely not the first thing we would want to say about marriage, particularly when making a proposal! Wright's new meaning leads us away from a framework of relationships and towards one of governance, away from a realm characterized by promise and faith to one where law and obedience are the determining features.

Such a shift in the covenant's primary significance allows Wright to overlook the role played by promise and faith in salvation, even though these are constitutive elements both of the covenant with Abraham and also of Paul's own thought. Speaking of the covenant with Abraham Paul writes: ' ... so that what was promised, being given through faith in Jesus Christ, might be given to those who believe' (Gal 3. 22b). A soteriology which has no place for the dynamic of promise and faith in salvation is bound to misrepresent the meaning of both Paul and of the covenant.

Gospel

Wright, as we saw above, holds that the gospel is the proclamation of the lordship of Christ[79] and develops his argument, at least in part, from the message of the 'good news' in Isaiah 40 and its relation to the announcement of the coming King.

> ... the Isaianic message always was about the enthronement of YHWH and the dethronement of pagan gods; about the victory of Israel and the fall of Babylon; about the arrival of the Servant King and the consequent coming of peace and justice.[80]

What is absent in this particular discussion is any consideration of what is meant by the opening verses of Isaiah 40, for these appear to offer a completely different perspective on the 'good news'.

> Comfort, comfort my people, says your God.
> Speak tenderly to Jerusalem, and proclaim to her
> that her hard service has been completed,
> that her sin has been paid for,
> that she has received from the Lord's hand
> double for all her sins (Isa 40. 1, 2).

---

[79] I am not suggesting that Wright was the originator of all the theological ideas in this scheme. E. P. Sanders gives emphasis to the lordship of Christ as the proper meaning of the atonement, but allows some space for mediatory elements: 'Thus the purpose of Christ's death was not simply to provide expiation, but that he might become Lord and thus save those who belong to him and are "in" him.' *Paul and Palestinian Judaism* (Minneapolis, Fortress Press, 1977), p. 465.

[80] Tom Wright, *What St Paul Really Said* (Oxford, Lion Publishing plc, 1997), p. 44.

Why the exile? Why had the Jews been taken into captivity? It is surely not to be explained by reference to the power of the pagan gods or the might of Babylon. The armies of the heathen king Cyrus were mere instruments used by God to serve his own purposes (Isa 45), whereas the pagan gods were considered to be no more than carved pieces of wood, unable to do anything and worthy of ridicule (Isa 41. 6–20). Difficult as it might be for our own age to comprehend, the exile came to be understood by the Jews as the judgement of God against their own covenant unfaithfulness. And it is through such knowledge that they survived and were transformed as a people. If we are to understand the implications for the Jews of the content of the 'good news' of a return from exile, we need first to share in their perception of the predicament which had befallen them:

> Cut off your hair and throw it away; take up a lament on the barren heights, for the Lord has rejected and abandoned this generation that is under his wrath (Jer 7. 29).

> The Lord has rejected his altar and abandoned his sanctuary. He has handed over to the enemy the walls of her palaces; they have raised a shout in the house of the Lord as on the day of an appointed feast (Lam 2: 7).

> And when the people ask, 'Why has God done all this to us?' you will tell them, 'As you have forsaken me and served foreign gods in your own land, so now you will serve foreigners in a land not your own' (Jer 5. 19).

To view the gods of the pagans and the might of armies of Babylon as the plight which faced the Jews in exile is to trivialize their experience and to miss the theological point completely. The 'good news' is in the first place about God's favour; it is about forgiveness and the restoration of relationships. This is the heart of its promise:

> 'For a brief moment I abandoned you, but with deep compassion I will bring you back. In a surge of anger I hid my face from you for a moment, but with everlasting kindness I will have compassion on you,' says the Lord your Redeemer (Isa 54. 7, 8).

Now Wright is fully aware of this perspective and develops it competently under a section entitled 'Covenant, Redemption and Forgiveness' in *The New Testament and the People of God* (pp. 272ff). His difficulty here is that such a view wholly undermines his theory that the gospel is simply about the 'lordship of Christ'. For if the predicament of the Jews has to do with the judgement of God on their unfaithfulness, then the exile is itself a manifestation of his divine lordship and power. Power and authority, of themselves, clearly do not bring hope for a people in such a condition. What the Jews long for is to hear the promise of divine mercy and forgiveness.

To maintain the neat simplicity of a soteriological system informed wholly by ideas of governance, Wright has to ignore the understanding of our predicament as divine judgement or an estrangement of our relationship with God. All we are then left with is a set of external enemies and these can be overcome by divine power, by the proclamation of God's majesty. Concepts of relationship are replaced by those of governance and the gospel is denuded of the ideas of mercy and absolution. Grace gives way to law.

It is appropriate at this point to outline our own understanding of the relationship of the proclamation of divine lordship to the gospel. We have seen from our study in the last chapter that in the announcement of the Kingdom of Heaven the good news lies not so much in its message of divine power and authority, as in its word of blessing to the poor in spirit; its promise of forgiveness to the guilty; its offer of mercy to the undeserving. The good news that formed the content of Peter's preaching had to do more with the promise of forgiveness and the Holy Spirit than the proclamation of the resurrection of Christ to a position of authority. The latter served, rather, to reveal to Peter's hearers the serious nature of their present predicament. In short, the proclamation of the lordship of Christ, or of the divine authority of God, is not of itself the gospel. It offers no hope to those who are estranged and in need of reconciliation. It does, of course, serve as the gospel's presupposition, illuminating the human predicament and so encouraging the hearer to seek mercy. It gives focus to the intention of the gospel to lead us to conformity to the divine will, and so to Christ himself, through the obedience of faith. It embodies the confession of faithfulness required of those who respond to the gospel. It reveals the eschatological goal of the gospel, the submission of every power and authority to the rule of Christ. But it is, of itself, not the gospel. It is not a message of salvation, for apart from other considerations it offers no hope of a gracious God for the ungodly, of forgiveness for the guilty, of mercy for the undeserving.

Atonement

There is, as we suggested above, a neat consistency about Wright's soteri-ology. It is uniformly shaped by the ideas of governance. As one might expect within such a system his interpretation of the atonement is deter-mined by the concepts of power, victory and order.

> When we ask how it was that Jesus' cruel death was the decisive victory over the powers, sin and death included, Paul at once replies: because it was the fulfilment of God's promise that through Abraham and his seed he would undo the evil in the world (*What St Paul Really Said*, p. 48). As we have just seen, Paul understands Jesus' execution as the moment when the creator's love wins the victory over the rebellious creation, when the forces that have enslaved humans and the world are defeated once and for all (p. 49). At the heart of Paul's gospel there stands the claim that the death of Jesus the king has defeated evil at its heart (p. 52).

It is not that Wright is unaware of the rich world of mediatorial ideas including reconciliation, forgiveness, mercy, ransom and sacrifice. They simply have no place within his interpretative framework, for the set of relationships which they imply undermines its rigid governmental structure. And so they are, by and large, either left aside or transformed in their meaning. Words like 'justification' and 'righteousness', which have had such rich significance for the Church these past two millennia in delineating the renewal of relationship, are incorporated into his scheme by having their primary meanings transposed into those of categorization[81] and governance.[82]

I would argue that Wright's soteriological model, based on the ideas of power and victory, does not work as an interpretive tool for an array of reasons. First, as we saw in the opening chapter, it clearly fails to give an adequate account of the most thorough presentation of the atonement in the Scriptures, that is, the argument of Paul in the first section of Romans. Second, it offers no solution to the primal human predicament either of the Jews in exile, living there as a consequence of their unfaithfulness to God, or of humankind as a whole, alienated from its creator and lying under his judgement. Third, although it provides a framework of thought where sin can be defeated as some sort of external enemy, it leaves unaddressed the actual sins in our lives and their devastating consequences, particularly on our world of relationships. The peace it offers is the aftermath of the destruction of all God's enemies, what one might call 'the Hiroshima effect', a sobering thought for those of us who have lived at enmity with God. The peace brought about through the atonement, however, is of a rather different sort:

> For God was pleased to have all his fullness dwell in him,
> and through him to reconcile to himself all things,
> whether things on earth or things in heaven,
> by making peace through his blood, shed on the cross.

The peace spoken of here has to do with reconciliation with God, with one another and with all of creation. It is the sort of peace that is brought about by a mediator not a SWAT team,[83] one whose holocaust has the fragrance of a lamb-offering rather than the smell of cordite.

---

[81] The idea of justification as categorization is central to Wright's argument. 'What Paul means by justification, in this context, should therefore be clear. It is not "how you become a Christian", so much as "how you can tell who is a member of the covenant family". *What St Paul Really Said*, p. 122.

[82] The idea of the righteousness of God as a way of ordering is apparent in the following passage: '...we discover that God's righteousness, seen in terms of covenant faithfulness and through the image of the lawcourt, was to be the instrument of putting the world to rights – of what we might call cosmic restorative justice.' N. T. Wright, *The Letter to the Romans: Introduction, Commentary and Reflection*, The New Interpreter's Bible, A Commentary in Twelve Volumes, vol. X (Nashville, Abingdon Press, 2002), p. 400.

[83] The Special Weapons Assault Team is a unit that has been formed in a number of police forces to deal decisively with hostage-takers when the process of negotiation or mediation is unproductive.

In Wright's model a system of governance, dependent on ideas like authority, order, victory and obedience, replaces a scheme informed by the concept of relationship and the ideas of accountability, confession, restoration, forgiveness, mercy and grace. We have seen how such a structure is unable to give an adequate explanation of the central features of the biblical material before it. Further than that, the removal of faith from the dynamic of salvation means the inevitable loss of the concept of promise or gift from the gospel. We are left with a somewhat bleak prospect, reminiscent of one that is forever winter and never Christmas.

Presenting the gospel

How can facts be put forward as promises? How do the events of the atonement become the content of a promise of salvation requiring our response? How does an evangelist like Paul actually present the gospel?

Although in Acts we have some summary accounts of Paul's preaching, we have no immediate access to his sermons. There are, however, one or two occasions in his correspondence where the form of his discussion moves surprisingly close to that of evangelistic proclamation. We might be able through one of these to catch a glimpse into the way he used to present the gospel to those who gathered to hear him in the market places and lecture rooms of those ancient Greek cities.

> All this is from God, who reconciled us to himself through Christ and gave us the ministry of reconciliation: that God was reconciling the world to himself in Christ, not counting men's sins against them. And he has committed to us the message of reconciliation. We are therefore Christ's ambassadors, as though God were making his appeal through us. We implore you on Christ's behalf: Be reconciled to God. God made him who had no sin to be sin for us, so that in him we might become the righteousness of God.(2 Cor 5. 18–21).

In this letter to the church in Corinth Paul finds himself forced to defend his ministry in the face of the alternate leadership style of certain visiting 'super-apostles'. He describes his ministry as one of reconciliation. In a world of enmity and estrangement, God is calling men and women to peace with himself. Paul sees himself as an agent of this divine appeal. Such 'peace' or 'reconciliation', if it is to be genuine, means dealing with the causes of alienation, putting aside past wrongs, cancelling old debts, forgiving sins. This is precisely what God has been doing (see v 19b).

Paul considers God's reconciling action with respect to three rather different groups:

1. God *has reconciled* us. The group Paul refers to includes himself, his fellow workers and possibly even the local Christian community. The aorist

tense signifies a completed event. Paul and his friends now know what it is to be at peace with God.

2. God *was reconciling* the world to himself. From Antioch, through Cyprus, across Asia Minor and into Europe, Paul had witnessed scores of people from all walks of life responding to his gospel message and receiving baptism into the Christian community. God had clearly been at work throughout this period reconciling to himself both Jews and Gentiles, slave and free, male and female. Paul uses the imperfect tense to indicate the ongoing nature of God's saving action in his ministry and that of his fellow evangelists.

3. *Be reconciled* to God. Let God's redemptive ministry continue! Some who hear this letter read in the churches will not yet have made their peace with God. The imperative mood indicates that a response is required of them and Paul makes it quite clear in the verses that follow that now is the appropriate time to do so. What is the actual content of the gospel promise to which they are being asked to respond?

It has two elements:

1. 'God made him who had no sin to be sin for us.' Commentators differ as to whether this should be translated as 'a sin offering' or simply as 'sin'.[84] Does it refer to Christ's role as a sacrificial offering for our sin or to his identification with our sins and the assumption of their consequences upon himself? Although I incline to the second, the difference is probably not material to this discussion. Christ in his person has died on our behalf, so that we might not have to die the death that sin deserves. This is a declaration of the atonement as an accomplished fact. This is the foundation of the gospel promise.

2. ... so that we might become the righteousness of God.' Paul puts forward the possibility of a right relationship or standing with God. It is a righteousness 'in him', suggesting that it is a righteousness that is received from participation in Christ's righteousness, a sharing in the standing that he has before God. It is also a righteousness of God in that God is its author. There are, of course, minor variations in the way some might interpret these words which do not affect the substance of the argument. What is clear is that a new status of complete and unqualified acceptance with God is being offered to the guilty, the godless and the undeserving on the basis of the atoning work of Christ. This is the promise of the gospel. It is the promise of peace with God.

How then are the hearers of this good news urged to respond? Paul begs them to 'be reconciled with God', today. If someone were to ask: 'How are we to do that?' it would suggest that they have probably failed to understand what is on offer. If your eyes have been opened to recognize the pearl of great value you will know what you must do to possess it. If you are aware that you

---

[84] See the discussion in Margaret E. Thrall, *The Second Epistle to the Corinthians*, vol. 1, The International Critical Commentary on the Holy Scriptures of the Old and New Testaments (T&T Clark, Edinburgh, 1994), pp. 439–44.

have in your hands the invitation to the king's banquet it will be clear how you should respond. The prodigal son returning to his family home did not have to be told *how* to be reconciled to his father, he simply allowed his father to embrace him with his love, clothe him with his cloak and own him by placing his ring on his finger. 'Be reconciled' has here the same function as 'believe'. It looks not to itself and its manifold inadequacy, but embraces the gift and more particularly the giver, for ultimately the two are one.

Conclusion

I began by asking: Why did God become man? It is, one could say, the philosophical equivalent of the question: What is Christianity all about? The answer took the form of a condensed narrative, what I have described as a master-story:

> *The Son became as we are so that he might, on our behalf, make peace with God.*

It encapsulates a mediatorial understanding of the atonement; one which we have contended is normative in that it gives a coherent account of the whole range of biblical metaphors and themes which refer to salvation.

This book has been written to defend that master-story, both from attack and from misunderstanding. In each of its chapters it became apparent that, despite the desire for brevity, the matter under consideration demanded that other perspectives be included in our response to the original question. And so the narrative evolved, for as we followed the logic of the enquiry what had been said before appeared not merely insufficient but sometimes distorting. Our response came to take the following shape:

> *The Father gave his only Son to become as we are so that, in offering up himself on our behalf through the Spirit, he might reconcile us to God.*

But the process was not to be stopped. We recognized that the saving work of the Holy Spirit in our own lives through promise and faith was itself an integral aspect of the story. It meant that as we came to the end of our study there was before us not so much a 'master-story' as an extended commentary on it, with so many important things still needing to be said. And perhaps that is all this book is: an unfinished commentary on this one-line narrative.

The passion that has driven the work is derived from the perceived significance of this particular story. Its value is reckoned to lie not merely in the coherence it might offer to one branch of academic theology. Nor is it simply a fresh reminder to the Church of the soil from which her faith has sprung. These few words are seen to include within themselves the essence of the gospel. To explain this gospel, sensitively and imaginatively, presenting it as promise in the power of the Spirit is the particular mission of the Church. Wherever she fails in this high calling her own life will surely wither away. But in her faithful fulfilment of it, lies the hope of the world, for it is through the gospel that the promised kingdom of peace will come.

Selected Bibliography

Anselm *Cur Deus Homo* (Edinburgh, John Grant, 1909)

Arminius, James, Works of J. Arminius (Grand Rapids, Christian Classics Ethereal Library, 2002)

Aquinas, Thomas, *The Summa Theologica*, trans. by Fathers of the English Dominican Province (Benziger Bros. edn, 1947)

Augustine, *A Treatise on the Grace of Christ and on Original Sin*, from A Select Library of the Nicene and Post-Nicene Fathers of the Christian Church, ed. by Philip Schaff, vol. 5 (Grand Rapids, Wm. B. Eerdmans)

Augustine, *A Treatise Concerning Man's Perfection in Righteousness*, from A Select Library of the Nicene and Post-Nicene Fathers of the Christian Church, ed. by Philip Schaff, vol 5 (Grand Rapids, Wm. B. Eerdmans, Grand Rapids)

Augustine, *Confessions* London, (Penguin Classics, 1977)

Augustine, *On the Trinity*, The Nicene and Post-Nicene Fathers, vol. 3 (Grand Rapids Michigan, Wm. B. Eerdmans, 1975ff.)

Augustine, *City of God*, The Nicene and Post-Nicene Fathers, vol. 6–2 (Grand Rapids Michigan, Wm. B. Eerdmans, 1975ff.)

Aulén, Gustaf, *Christus Victor: An historical study of the three main types of the idea of the Atonement*, trans. by A. G. Hebert, (London, SPCK, 1978)

Baillie, D. M., *God was in Christ: An Essay on Incarnation and Atonement* (London, Faber & Faber Ltd, 1966)

Barth, Karl, *Church Dogmatics*, 2nd edn, ed. by G. W. Bromiley & T. F. Torrance (Edinburgh, T&T Clark, 1980)

Barth, Karl, *The Epistle to the Romans*, trans. from the 6th edn by Edwyn C. Hoskyns (London, Oxford University Press, 1932)

Brunner, Emil, *The Mediator: A Study of the Central Doctrine of the Christian Faith*, trans. by Olive Wyon (London, Lutterworth Press, 1942)

Bultmann, Rudolf, *Theology of the New Testament*, vol. 1 (London, SCM Press Ltd, 1965)

Calvin, John, *Institutes of Christian Religion*, trans. by Henry Beveridge (Grand Rapids, Michigan, William B. Eerdmans, 1970)

Campbell, John McLeod, *The Nature of the Atonement and its relation to Remission of Sins and Eternal Life*, 5th edn (London, Macmillan & Co., 1878)

Courtenay, William, 'Nominalism', in *A New Dictionary of Christian Theology*, ed. by Alan Richardson & John Bowden, (London, SCM Press Ltd, 1985)

Cranfield, C. E. B., *The Epistle to the Romans*, vol. 1, International Critical Commentary on the Holy Scriptures of the Old and New Testaments (Edinburgh, T&T Clark Ltd, 1980)

Denny, James, *The Death of Christ* (London, Tyndale Press, 1956)

Dillistone, F. W., *The Christian Understanding of the Atonement* (London, SCM Press Ltd, 1984)

Dodd, C. H., '*HILASKESTHAI*, Its Cognates, Derivatives, and Synonyms, in the Septuagint', *Journal of Theological Studies*, xxxii (July 1931)

Dodd, C. H., *The Apostolic Preaching and its Developments* (London, Hodder & Stoughton, 1936)

Forsyth, P. T., *The Person and Place of Jesus Christ* (London, United Reformed Church, 1999)

Gunton, Colin E, *The Actuality of the Atonement: A study of Metaphor, Rationality and the Christian Tradition* (Edinburgh, T&T Clark, 1988)

Gunton, Colin E., *The Christian Faith: An Introduction to Christian Doctrine* (Oxford, Blackwell Publishers, 2002)

Hanson, A. T., *The Wrath of the Lamb* (London, SPCK, 1957)

Hays, Richard B., '*PISTIS* and Pauline Christology: What is at stake?' *Pauline Theology*, vol. 4, ed. by E. Elizabeth Johnson & David M. Hay (Atlanta, Georgia, Scholars Press, 1997)

Horton, Michael S., *Lord and Servant: A Covenant Christology* (Louisville, WJK, 2005)

Hume, David, *Enquiries concerning Human Understanding and concerning the Principles of Morals*, 3rd edn (Oxford, Oxford University Press, 1978)

Kähler, Martin, *The so-called Historical Jesus and the Historic Biblical Christ*, trans. by Carl E. Braaten (Philadelphia: Fortress Press, 1964)

Kelly, J. N. D., *Early Christian Doctrines*, 5th edn, (London, Adam & Charles Black, 1977)

Longenecker, Richard N. (ed.), *The Road from Damascus: The Impact of Paul's Conversion on His Life, Thought, and Ministry* (Grand Rapids, Michigan, William B. Eerdmans, 1997)

Luther, Martin, *Commentary on the Epistle to the Romans*, trans. by J.Theodore Mueller, (Grand Rapids, Michigan, Zondervan Publishing House, 1954)

Luther, Martin, *Selections from his Writings*, ed. by John Dillenberger (New York, Anchor Books, 1961)

McGrath, Alister E., *Justitia Dei, A History of the Christian Doctrine of Justification*, 2nd edn (Cambridge, Cambridge University Press, 1998)

Martin, Ralph P., *Reconciliation: A study of Paul's theology* (London, Marshall, Morgan & Scott, 1981)

Moltmann, Jürgen, *The Crucified God*, trans. by R. A. Wilson & John Bowden (London, SCM Press, 2001)

Moltmann, Jürgen, *The Trinity and the Kingdom of God: The doctrine of God*, trans. by Margaret Kohl (London, SCM Press, 1981)

Morris, Leon, *The Apostolic Preaching of the Cross* (London, Tyndale Press, 1960)

Murray, John, *Redemption, Accomplished and Applied* (London, Banner of Truth Trust, 1961)

Murray, John, *The Epistle to the Romans* (London, Marshall, Morgan & Scott, 1960)

Owen, John, *A Declaration of the Glorious Mystery of the Person of Christ*, vol. 1, The Works of John Owen, ed. by William H. Goold (London, Banner of Truth Trust, 1965)

Owen, John, *A Discourse concerning the Holy Spirit*, vol. 3, The Works of John Owen ed. by William H. Goold (London, Banner of Truth Trust, 1965)

Owen John, *The Death of Death in the Death of Christ*, vol. 10, The Works of John Owen, ed. by William H Goold, (London, Banner of Truth Trust, 1965–8)

Owen, John, *The Doctrine of the Saints' Perseverance Explained and Confirmed*, vol. 11, The Works of John Owen, ed. by William H. Goold, (London, Banner of Truth Trust, 1965–8)

Pannenberg, Wolfhart, *Jesus: God and Man* (London, SCM Press, 1985)

Sanders, E. P., *Paul and Palestinian Judaism: A Comparison of Patterns of Religion* (London, SCM Press, 1977)

Schleiermacher, F., *The Christian Faith* (Edinburgh, T&T Clark, 1976)

Schweitzer, Albert, *The Quest of the Historical Jesus* (London, SCM Press Ltd, 1981)

Sölle, Dorothée, *Christ the Representative: An Essay in Theology after the 'Death of God'*, trans. by D. Lewis (London, SCM Press, 1967)

Spence, Alan, 'Christ's humanity and ours: John Owen' in *Persons, Divine and Human*, ed, by Christoph Schwöbel & Colin E. Gunton (Edinburgh, T&T Clark, 1991)

Stott, John, *The Cross of Christ* (London, Inter-Varsity Press, 1996)

Thrall, Margaret E., *The Second Epistle to the Corinthians*, vol.1 International Critical Commentary on the Holy Scriptures of the Old and New Testaments (Edinburgh, T&T Clark, 1994)

Torrance, James B., *Worship, Community and the Triune God of Grace* (Carlisle, Paternoster Press, 1996)

Torrance, T. F., *God and Rationality* (London, Oxford University Press, 1971)

Torrance, T. F., *The Mediation of Christ*, rev. edn (Edinburgh, T&T Clark, 1992)

Watson, Thomas, *A Body of Divinity* (London, Banner of Truth Trust, 1965)

Whale, J. S., *Victor and Victim: The Christian Doctrine of Redemption* (Cambridge, Cambridge University Press, 1960)

Wright, N. T., *Jesus and the Victory of God* (London, SPCK, 1996)

Wright, N. T., *The Climax of the Covenant: Christ and the Law in Pauline Theology* (Minneapolis, Fortress Press, 1993)

Wright, N. T., *The Letter to the Romans: Introduction, Commentary and Reflection*, The New Interpreter's Bible, A Commentary in Twelve Volumes, vol. 10 (Nashville, Abingdon Press, 2002)

Wright, N. T., *The New Testament and the People of God* (Minneapolis, Fortress Press, 1992)

Wright, Tom, *What St Paul Really Said* (Oxford, Lion Publishing plc, 1997)

Young, Frances, *Sacrifice and the Death of Christ* (London, SPCK, 1975)

Index

9 780567 031181